A Way Out

"If you're not sure if your business will survive, feel lost right now, or just want to get more out of the life you're living – this book is for you. During this otherwise perfect storm of stress, panic, and fear, A Way Out guides you down a new path to true success, peace, and prosperity through simple actionable steps backed by years of science and research. I've already put several quotes from it on my inspiration wall."

– Jennifer Jolly, Nationally Syndicated Tech-Life Columnist, Founder Techish.com.

"No one has ever become poor by giving."

– Anne Frank

A Way Out

The Hidden Fortune of Service

KRIS CHETTAYAR

Columbus, Ohio

A Way Out: The Hidden Fortune of Service

Published by Gatekeeper Press
2167 Stringtown Rd, Suite 109
Columbus, OH 43123-2989
www.GatekeeperPress.com

Copyright © 2021 by IgnitionPoint, LLC
All rights reserved. Neither this book, nor any parts within it may be sold or reproduced in any form or by any electronic or mechanical means, including information storage and retrieval systems without permission in writing from the author. The only exception is by a reviewer, who may quote short excerpts in a review.

Library of Congress Control Number: 2020944611

ISBN (hardcover): 9781662904189
ISBN (paperback): 9781662904196
eISBN: 9781662904202

Matthew 7:12

Contents

The Story Behind the Book

I spent most of my career helping companies build products and services to serve the needs of everyday consumers like you and me. In the process, I became an expert at identifying the determinants of new product success, and the sales and marketing programs to promote them. In fact, during the course of my career, I analyzed petabytes of data across thousands of programs in order to identify the critical success factors (CSF) that lead to success so I could use it to make more money.

From all the data I analyzed, it became clear to me that a "service mentality," and the act of service itself, was at the heart of success in any business endeavor. However, I wondered if a service mentality had a similar impact on personal success. So, I set course to find out.

The year was 2008 when I conducted a proprietary research study to determine if being service oriented (i.e. other focused) could explain why one person had a greater personal net worth compared to someone who might be struggling financially. In the study, I asked 185 consumers to complete the Interpersonal Reactivity Index Survey, which measures people's levels of empathy and their ability to understand the perspectives of other people. The results of the study were surprising.

I discovered that people who had the highest net worth also scored higher in their ability to identify the needs of others. These people were better off because they used their insight to profit in various ways. At this point, it became clear to me that service was also at the heart of personal success.

This insight made me recall my days in graduate school, studying economic theory, and the words of Adam Smith, the great architect of modern-day capitalism. Smith proposed that when people are pursuing their own interests, they would branch out and build products and services for other people, which would make them rich. However, the byproduct of this seemingly self-interested pursuit was that society benefited from these entrepreneurs who serve people. That is, all of society was made richer by a person's efforts to serve other people. This seemed like a hidden precept to me, and one that was forgotten in many defunct government and philanthropic efforts.

At the same time I had this insight, I witnessed a ballooning U.S. government debt nearing 10 trillion dollars to fund many noble programs. Yet, somehow, I thought we had forgotten what made America great and it wasn't more government spending. What made America great was the service mentality of its citizens and its market economy, but I'm not a politician focused on government programs, so I just went back to my research.

This time I broadened and expanded my research focus by exploring if there were any benefits of service beyond the obvious economic ones. I was astonished to learn that service to others had a profound impact in many areas of life I did not expect. I learned that service has a substantial impact on fighting diseases, and that even witnessing an act of service would raise the level of immunoglobulin A in your blood, which fights bacteria and viruses. I also uncovered additional research that showed service was a natural remedy to combat depression and anger because it increases levels of natural opiates. I labeled this the do-good feel-good phenomenon.

The list of benefits was growing, and the power of service became clear to me. However, it had taken me two master's degrees, 15 years of professional experience, and millions of dollars in market research to figure it out. It all seemed like my little secret, and I didn't think much about it until The Great Recession hit. It was then I felt I had to share what I discovered. I felt I needed to do something to help.

I began writing *A Way Out: The Hidden Fortune of Service* in late 2008 with the express purpose of helping people and businesses struggling with the economic and emotional impact of a financial system teetering on the brink of collapse. By the time I was done with the book, it was 2011 and the entire world was coming out of the other side of The Great Recession in what would lead to the "Great Bull Run" in the stock market and one of the longest streaks of economic growth ever seen. By then, it seemed my book had little relevance on the scale I had imagined it. So, I placed the book on the shelf, and I forgot about it.

In January of 2020 I felt something deep inside tell me it was time to publish *A Way Out*. This year, I felt, the book was going to be important, so I pulled it off the shelf and began editing it. Then, in February 2020, COVID-19 hit, and all hell broke loose. *The Great Repression* had begun.

People were dying. The stock market collapsed. Soon thereafter we were in social lockdown, businesses were forced to close, and unemployment was spiking to levels not seen since The Great Depression. I watched people everywhere desperate, wondering how they were going to get by and survive.

I kept editing *A Way Out* until it was finally ready to be published. And though it's 2021, I did my best to get it out as fast as I could. However, the value of *A Way Out* transcends the immediate ills we face. The book provides a blueprint for people and businesses to use in any economic circumstance to survive and thrive.

When things go wrong, it's not over. There is a solution. There is *A Way Out*!

Introduction

The year is 2021, and the entire world is in the midst of what many are calling *The Great Repression* brought upon by a global pandemic. National and local governments have placed us into a social lockdown to control the spread of COVID-19 and the tragedy it has brought to countless victims. The result of these measures has slowed the spread of the disease, but it has come at a severe economic cost.

The closure of mass businesses deemed non-essentials have resulted in a scale of employee layoffs that hasn't occurred since The Great Depression. Individuals and businesses everywhere are left in desperate circumstances, uncertain if they will be able to survive these challenging times. Yet, all is not lost.

There is A *Way Out*.

If you are searching for a solution to improve your situation, then I assure you that you will find it in this book. I used the mindset and practices in this book to turn my own life around and succeed amid challenging economic circumstances. I also used what I learned to help companies build new products and services to transform and grow their business. You can use the mindset and principles to change your situation, too.

During the past twenty years, I have worked to deepen my understanding of what skills lead to success in career and business. My journey led me down some winding and often divergent paths into academia, the applied sciences, and the trenches of corporate America as a consultant and executive for some of the most respected brand names in business.

The central philosophy governing my academic pursuits was framed by the famous management consultant, Peter Drucker.

He wrote, "Because its purpose is to create a customer, the business has two—and only two—functions: marketing and innovation. Marketing and innovation create value. All the rest are costs[1]."

I set out to hone my skills, accordingly. I went on to earn a Master's Degree in Marketing and a Master's Degree in Product Development, both from Northwestern University. But my efforts to identify the "magic formula" for generating lots of value for myself and others didn't end in the classroom.

In the applied sciences, I conducted myriad market research studies to understand customer behavior, how to serve customer needs, and how to identify the critical success factors that motivate people to buy products and services. Those insights helped me understand how to drive value in the marketplace.

In business, I led customer-service teams, launched marketing programs, and innovated new products, all of which have generated hundreds of million dollars in revenue and

---

1 (Trout, 2006)

earnings. That experience gave me an inside track into what works and what doesn't when it comes to driving value.

With the experiences I have gained in my career, I have concluded that success, either in life or in business, comes down to how good you are at serving the needs of others.

It's that simple.

When you provide great service to people, they reward you for it. This is proven by the success of individuals, companies, and even national economies.

You will achieve success in life when, and only when, you focus on serving the needs of others. In fact, if you adopt a business perspective and start serving everyone like a customer, then you can achieve super success.

I am not the only person who has made this connection. Many successful people have also identified with this principle, and some have written about it. However, through a lot of research, I have identified many hidden benefits to an around-the-clock service mentality that does more than improve customer satisfaction.

Serving everyone like a customer will have profound impact in every area of your personal and professional life. How? As you'll learn, it builds mental acuity that can help you become sensitive to the needs of others. This sensitivity will help you to innovate new products, improve productivity, and grow income. In addition, the act of service itself will do more to improve physical health and increase emotional well-being than just about anything else.

A Way Out: The Hidden Fortune of Service will help you discover the power of service, educate you on all the benefits, and provide you with strategies for applying skills that will lead to success.

If you use what you learn in this book, you will find a way to succeed-no matter your current circumstances. I guarantee it!

Chapter 1

The Success Paradox

Your life *is* your *business*. And just like any business, you want to profit from your actions. You want to be wealthy, healthy, and happy. All of these are noble goals.

You will achieve all of these goals when, and only when, you serve the needs of others. That may seem counterintuitive, but it's true, nonetheless. I call this the "success paradox."

Consider this: the majority of the richest one hundred people in the world didn't inherit their money or make it in the stock market. They may have sold a product, provided a service, or provided a natural resource to amass their wealth. Whatever the method is, the source is the same. The rich got that way because they served the needs of many, many people.

During the Great Recession of 2007, Carlos Slim surpassed Bill Gates as the world's richest person. His net worth was estimated at $74 billion at the time[2]. How did he get that rich? He built businesses that served the needs of a lot of different people.

2 (Forbes, 2020)

A large portion of Slim's wealth came from his acquisition of the Mexican telephone company Telemex in 1990. In order to bolster the sales at Telemex, Slim created a prepaid wireless service for customers. Initially the executives at Telemex were against the plan, but it turned out that Slim's idea filled an enormous need. The prepaid wireless service has helped grow the Telemex customer base by sixty-six percent every year for fifteen years[3].

During The Great Repression of 2020, Jeff Bezos became the new richest person in the world. Jeff amassed his $187 billion net worth from the stock he owns in the company he built to serve online shoppers[4].

During the majority of 2020, people turned to online shopping to buy the products they needed. Amazon's system of logistics became a critical infrastructure to help millions of people survive the social lock down imposed by governments around the world. As a result, people spent their money with Amazon, which in turn made Jeff a rich man.

It pays to serve.

Providing service is the only way to achieve super-success in your personal or business life. If that's what you want, then you should do as the rich do and find a way to serve as many people as possible.

The Formula for Success: Serve the Most People Possible

---

[3] (Carlos Slim Helu, n.d.)

[4] (Kiersz & Rogers, 2020)

Top 25 Richest People in the World, 2020[5]

Rank	Name	Networth	Source	Location
1	Jeff Bezos	$187 billion	Technology	United States
2	Bill Gates	$121 billion	Technology	United States
3	Mark Zuckerberg	$102 billion	Technology	United States
4	Mukesh Ambani	$80.6 billion	Energy	India
5	Bernard Arnault	$80.2 billion	Consumer	France
6	Warren Buffett	$79.2 billion	Diversified	United States
7	Steve Ballmer	$76.4 billion	Technology	United States
8	Larry Page	$71.3 billion	Technology	United States
9	Sergey Brin	$69.1 billion	Technology	United States
10	Elon R Musk	$68.7 billion	Technology	United States
11	Francoise Meyers	$65.6 billion	Consumer	France
12	Larry Ellison	$64.5 billion	Technology	United States
13	MacKenzie Scott	$60.9 billion	Technology	United States
14	Rob Walton	$57.9 billion	Retail	United States
15	Jim Walton	$57.7 billion	Retail	United States
16	Alice Walton	$57.1 billion	Retail	United States
17	Amancio Ortega	$56.8 billion	Retail	Spain
18	Charles Koch	$56.1 billion	Industrial	United States
19	Julia Flesher Koch	$56.1 billion	Industrial	United States
20	Michael Bloomberg	$54.9 billion	Media and Telecom	United States
21	Pony Ma	$53.0 billion	Technology	China
22	Jack Ma	$50.7 billion	Technology	China
23	Carlos Slim	$45.7 billion	Diversified	Mexico
24	Jacqueline Mars	$41.1 billion	Food and Beverage	United States
25	John Mars	$41.1 billion	Food and Beverage	United States

Your success depends on your ability to serve others. So, if you don't have what you want, you probably haven't made service a priority in your life. Fortunately, it's never too late to change.

[5] (Papadoloulos, 2020)

Dedicated focus on the needs of others is the starting point of your personal and professional success. In fact, I proved the case in a proprietary research study I conducted some years ago.

In my research study, I selected a stratified random sample of 185 people in the U.S. to complete the Interpersonal Reactivity Index Survey. This survey measured people's level of interpersonal concern on four dimensions: perspective taking, fantasy scale, empathic concern, and personal distress.

The people who had a higher net worth had a higher interpersonal perspective of other's needs. That means, those who scored higher in the ability to see people's perspectives and needs, were worth more compared to those who scored lower on the test.

We have to serve other people if we want financial success. The most profitable companies understand this point. They know that the source of their profit is not the actual products themselves; it's the customer. The best companies know service is the critical success factor in business. A closer look at a customer satisfaction survey results makes this point clear.

BusinessWeek magazine and market research firm JD Power & Associates, partner each year to rate companies with the best customer service. The rating is based on a survey that consumers complete about the perceived quality of a company's staff and their customer-service processes[6]. The results identify the "Top 25 Customer Service Champs," which are identified and published annually in *BusinessWeek* magazine[7].

From 2005 to 2009, the publicly traded companies on the list of the "Top 25 Customer Champs" had average annualized earnings growth of 2.2 percent. In contrast, the S&P 500 suffered a decline of 7.3 percent. Although these returns don't seem like much, do

6 (Business Week, n.d.)

7 (Business Week, n.d.)

consider that this time period was smack dab in the middle of The Great Recession. While most companies were struggling to survive, those who provided the best service remained on solid footing.

In another study, the Strategic Management Institute documented the various strategies and profit impact of over three thousand businesses across all industries. Analysis of this data revealed that companies that provide the best quality services to their customers had an average return on investment of thirty percent, while those with the lowest quality, had an average return of five percent[8]. This finding suggests that by putting the needs of the customers first, you can dramatically change the profitability of your business. The same principle applies in your personal and professional life.

So, with all the potential benefits of service, what exactly does it mean?

I define service as the tangible and intangible things we do for others to deliver value. That could include the care with which we engineer a product, or it could mean the emotional or social sensitivity we exhibit when we deliver it. This definition broadens the scope of service and establishes it as a critical imperative to success because it is—and that's a fact, as noted above.

The salient benefit of good service is gaining a financial reward. You provide good service, and people will pay you for it. The more people you serve, the more money you make.

This is how fortunes are built. You too can make your fortune when you learn to serve the needs of many people.

But money isn't the only benefit of service. Other important byproducts of service are often overlooked. For one, service may lengthen your life. Research has shown that people who volunteer live longer than those who do not[9].

---

8 (Business Week, n.d.)

9 (Grimm, Spring, & Dietz, 2007)

Other research shows that people who serve others are able to fight off many diseases. Some medical studies even suggest a link between service and weight loss. Sounds crazy, I know, but it's true. We'll discuss more about this in a later chapter.

Providing great service will also do more to lengthen your relationships (personal, professional, and otherwise) compared to any other method. For instance, research shows that the best predictor of keeping a customer is based on how likely they are to recommend your service to someone else[10].

When customers recommend a company, they do so because they have been transformed into brand zealots. These zealots will go so far as to promote a service and by doing so, they create a social commitment to it that is hard to break. In social psychology, we know this phenomenon as the commitment and consistency principle.

The Commitment and Consistency Principle explains why people are loyal to something or someone after they promote it.

Great service tends to create positive word of mouth, which is usually far more effective than traditional forms of marketing. In the age of social media, service is one of the best marketing strategies you can use. Give great service, and you'll get people to "like you."

Although service is critical to your success, it is not something you can turn on and off. We have to constantly practice service in order to see its benefits. When you are constantly serving, you literally cause a psychological and physiological change in your mind and nervous system which in turn helps improve your ability

10 (Reichheld, 2001)

to spot and serve needs. The more you serve, the better you will become at identifying needs.

The ability to spot the needs of customers and serve them is how fortunes are made. This is how Jeff Bezos and Carlos Slim became the world's richest men, and this is how Amazon became one of the largest corporations in the world. By doing the same thing, you, too, can get rich, if that's what you want.

That's why serving everyone as if they were a customer leads to The success paradox.

Fortunes are lost when we fail to tune in to and serve the needs of others. Misplaced focus on your needs is why one person stays at the same level while others advance all around him. This is why one individual can never keep a job and another always has more job offers than she knows what to do with. It's why one person is miserable, while others are happy, healthy, and wealthy.

Without a dedicated focus on service, we eventually become morally bankrupt. We no longer care about people unless they can do something for us. We develop a situational value system, and we lose our ability to empathize. This weakens our ability to succeed, as well as weakening our community.

When Money is the Focus

The Great Recession in the U.S. was caused by a lack of empathy, more or less. Certain financial companies sold mortgages to people who couldn't afford the loan. These companies didn't care though because they packaged the loans in bonds and sold them to investors risk-free. When interest rates began to rise, homeowners defaulted, and investors lost money. Investors then sold their stocks and bonds; people cut spending out of fear of the declining stock market and businesses laid off / pink-slipped employees. Everyone suffered.

When we are focused on serving people and providing value, we all benefit. Think of Apple, Inc. and the iPhone. The iPhone has improved our life. It has given us the ability to stay connected, interact, and even shop by using a simple and intuitive interface. It is an important tool for many of us, and it created the potential to sell us "apps." As a result, the iPhone has spawned thousands of new business opportunities for entrepreneurs, which creates jobs and strengthens our society. Everyone wins.

The success of your life, your business, and your community will depend on how well you can employ a customer-service orientation.

It all starts with you.

Chapter 2

The Hidden Fortune of Service

You will improve your fortune when you learn to serve. But what is your fortune?

Fortune can be your wealth, your luck, or your destiny. It can be any of these things or all of these things, but one thing is for sure—your fortune is always tied to serving people.

To build your fortune, you have to know the rules of service and use them to your advantage. Certain universal and immutable rules of life govern our fortune. Following them brings us good fortune, breaking them brings us bad fortune. One such rule comes in many forms but can be found in every culture of the world. Perhaps you have guessed it already. It's the Golden Rule.

Following the Golden Rule has great significance, much of which you probably never fully appreciated. But what does the Golden Rule really mean? I had a professor in college who told me, "the Golden Rule means he who has the gold, rules." That's a twisted way of thinking about it, but we all have our own interpretation.

Let's consider this together. What does it mean to "Do unto others as you would have them do unto you"?

Some people think it means treating people the way you would like to be treated, which is a reasonable understanding. But how you interpret this rule is partly subjective. To follow the Golden Rule, I'd reason that one must truly understand the needs and wants of others and then try to serve those needs and wants. It does no good to me if you simply do for me what you want and forget my likes, or vice versa.

If we want to be successful in any area of life, we need to understand a person's needs and wants and then serve that person in such a way as to be unique and specific to that individual—that is, serve people the way they want to be served. That's what we would want people to do for us, and that is the meaning of *Do unto others as you would have them do unto you.* This interpretation forms a philosophical foundation of creating value for yourself and others.

You'll improve your fortune when you serve everyone as if they were your customer. The evidence is all around you. You can see it in the relative performance of economies, of businesses, and even of the wealthiest individuals.

Economies

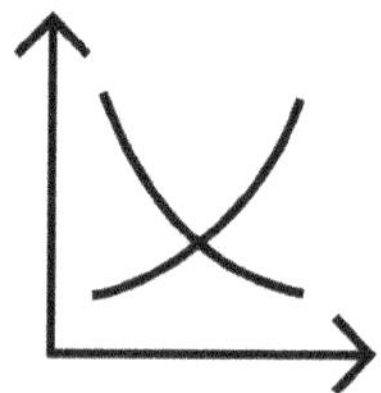

Let's examine the two major economic theories— capitalism and socialism—to see how serving everyone like a customer can impact an entire nation. We'll consider socialism first.

Socialism is characterized by public ownership of virtually all property resources. A central planning board makes all economic decisions, including the level of resource use, the composition and distribution of output, and the organization of production. The government owns all of the businesses, and those businesses operate according to state directives.

The Soviet Union's economy was Socialist. Where are they today? They are wiped off the map. Why? The buyer or consumer is not the center of a socialist system. The government is.

A central planning board determines how best to allocate resources, what products the consumer needs, and the appropriate quantities for serving those needs.

Can a central planning board accurately estimate your or my needs, wants, and desires? This system places all of the control in the hands of a small group of people who are somehow supposed to know what the masses want. More importantly, it produces things that don't work and products that don't sell.

According to former Soviet economists, only ten percent of Soviet finished goods were able to compete with their Western counterparts, and the average consumer faced long waiting periods to buy major appliances or furniture[11].

Comrades faced long waiting lines to buy anything. Buying the basics like food and other essentials was no exception. The burden of waiting in lines fell to the women, who received little assistance from their spouse and even less from the male-dominated society.

Soviet women were generally overstressed. As a consequence of the domestic pressure, the Soviet Union had high rates of abortion, alcoholism, and divorce[12].

This type of system forces the customer to bear unimaginable stress to purchase substandard products. Who wants to wait in line for shoddy products and services?

---

11 (htt)

12 (httl)

The same might be said about how you serve everyone. Are you forcing people to wait in line to get your inferior service? In other words, are you forcing people in your life to wait for poor treatment caused by a disregard for their needs and wants? How long can that last before you fall the way the Soviet Union did?

Capitalism, in contrast to socialism, is characterized by the private ownership of resources and the use of a system of markets and prices to coordinate and direct economic activity. In such a system, each participant is motivated by his or her self-interests, and each participant seeks to maximize income through individual decision-making. The market system functions as a mechanism through which individual decisions and preferences are communicated and coordinated[13].

Adam Smith is the architect of modern capitalism and free markets as written in his book, *The Wealth of Nations.* He argued that when people maximize their self-interests, they will branch out to develop goods and services for other people which in turn generates wealth for themselves and society as a whole. Precisely. This is The Hidden Fortune of Service.

Adam Smith:
The Father of Modern Economics and Capitalism[14]

[13] (McConnell & Brue, 1993)

[14] (htt2)

In a capitalist system, the customers, not a central planning board, decide what they want. The economy of the United States of America is based primarily on a capitalist system.

The customer has the upper hand in a capitalist system—and rightfully so. The customer has the money! And they *vote with their dollars* for the products that will succeed in the market. This system ensures that the needs of the customers are met and oftentimes exceeded. As such, the capitalist system seems to be superior to socialism.

But what about China? China now has the second-largest economy in the world, and they are a communist society. That's true. However, China achieved that growth by adopting capitalist principles. China's economy is now a form of state capitalism, which means the government owns an interest in private enterprise. But the goal of the enterprise is to maximize profits by serving customers.

China made all the people of the world their customers by manufacturing products as a low-cost producer. The world in turn, responded with its money.

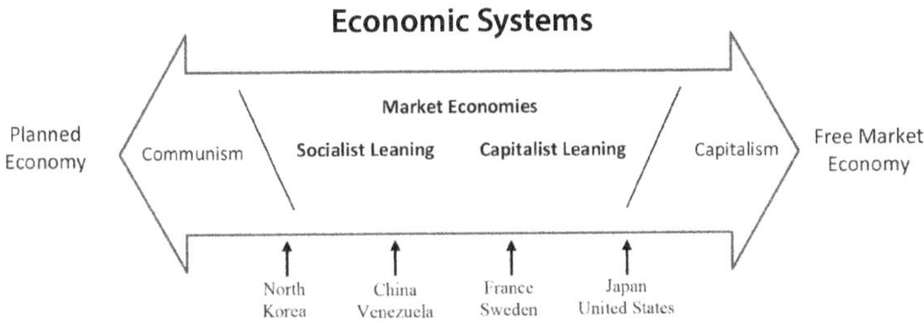

If you want to have a dramatic turnaround in your economy, you have to focus on serving markets and people the way China does. Increased job creation and wealth creation is the Hidden Fortune of Service. Indeed, we only have to consider the gross national product of the U.S. and the former Soviet Union to see the stark differences in industry and wealth between capitalism and socialism.

Gross national product (GNP) is the total value of all goods and services produced in a country in a year, including net income from investments in other countries[15]. It measures how much value a nation has been able to create.

Because of the way it is calculated, it allows economists and businesspeople to make comparisons among the nations.

The GNP for the Soviet Union in 1988 grew by 1.5 percent, and industrial output rose by 2.4 percent, according to the 1989 CIA *World Factbook*[16]. Total GNP was $2.5 trillion, which translates to about $8,700 per capita for the 288.7 million who lived in the Soviet Union at the time. Let's compare this performance to that of the United States of America.

The GNP for the U.S. grew at 3.8 percent, and the industrial output was five percent. Total GNP was $4.8 trillion, which translates to $19,900 per capita for the 248.2 million people who lived in the U.S. then.

The contrasts between socialism and capitalism are significant. In the socialist system, the organization comes first and the customer comes last. As a result, the customer and the organization lose part of their Fortune.

In capitalism, the customer comes first and the company that does the best job serving the customer, thrives. In this system, a successful business places its focus on serving the needs of the customer. Which then in turn, benefits the business. The same type of good fortune can accrue to you when you serve everyone like a customer.

15 (Microsoft Encarta College Dictionary, 2001)

16 (theodora.com, n.d.)

If you focus on serving needs, both you and society will benefit in measurable ways. Yet some countries and well-intentioned people do not do enough to stress this point in their doctrine, and the consequence of it is often disastrous.

One of the most respected economists of our time, Milton Friedman, said, "There is one and only one social responsibility of business — to use its resources and engage in activities designed to increase its profits so long as it stays within the rules of the game, which is to say, engages in open and free competition without deception or fraud."[17]

Friedman's doctrine have pervaded modern economic theory, and they were the basis of much of the fiscal policy during Ronald Reagan's presidency.

While no one can dispute Friedman's contributions to modern economic theory, one wonders if businesses should really be singularly focused on maximizing profits even if they do indeed play by the rules of the game. Why? Sometimes the rules, well, are bad rules.

The Great Recession, as it has come to be known, has shown us the impact of an illiberal emphasis on maximizing profits. Consider the root cause of the U.S. financial problems during 2008 to 2012: Some financial companies sought to maximize profits by lending money to people to buy homes that they couldn't afford. But these companies didn't care much because they *securitized the loans*, meaning they packaged the loans into something like a stock or bond, and then sold it to investors who, in turn, sold it to other investors. Rating agencies affirmed the quality of the bonds which made it seem like a good investment to investors.

These financial companies made enormous profits while they assumed virtually no risk, so they kept lending money. Easy

---

17 (Forswearing Greed, 2009)

money brought new consumers into the market to buy homes, and that caused a real estate bubble.

Along came other financial companies that provided a sort of insurance on those mortgage-backed securities just in case the homeowners started to default. Providing this insurance looked like easy money, so even municipalities in Australia invested in this scheme. Who would have guessed that so many people would not be able to make their mortgage payments?

When mortgage rates started rising, the borrowers started defaulting on their loans. Then the investors in the mortgage-backed securities started to lose money, so they claimed their insurance, which forced companies like Lehman Brothers to pay out large sums of money. Lehman started to lose big and finally collapsed. That set off a massive stock market sell-off, which in turn caused consumers to pull back on spending, leading to the worst recession in a generation. The irony is that many of the financial companies and mortgage lenders who helped create this mess imploded.

The responsibility of business is not to maximize profits in isolation. When profit is the only focus, the result of doing so in a deregulated market ensures that the company may eventually kill itself and perhaps the entire economy.

The sustainable purpose of business is to find, serve, and keep a profitable customer. By this definition, the business is still in business to make money, as it should be. However, it's in business to make money from customers not just once, but for as long as possible. That means it has to provide value and quality and act with integrity (moral rules), while also be a good law-abiding citizen (legal rules).

An individual or a company must put the needs, safety, and well-being of customers as its paramount concern. This philosophy promotes the welfare of the individual, the company, and society as a whole.

Case in point: An economics study in the 1990s found that when a society has more entrepreneurs who branch out to start companies and serve customers, these people not only benefit themselves, but the wealth of the society grows, as well.

In contrast, when society is dominated by professions such as finance and law that do nothing to create wealth, the effect is lower productivity, fewer technological opportunities, and slower economic growth[18]. Bear in mind that just before the collapse of the financial markets in 2008, the proportion of U.S. workers in finance was at an all-time high.

The financial sector serves a purpose, but by itself it does nothing to create wealth. The emphasis of finance is to make money. And when people are focused only on money, the odds increase for crime, corruption, and financial catastrophe. In response, the government has no choice but to establish rules and consequences to regulate the markets and protect the innocent from unscrupulous people.

When companies exist to profitably maximize the value of customers, the need for regulation is diminished. The market regulates itself.

Business

One of the largest companies in the world is WalMart. The WalMart company generated $524 billion in 2020, a staggering

18 (Bannon, 2009)

amount of money. So how did WalMart do it? Besides being a very well-run organization, it has placed you and me at the center of their strategy.

WalMart is dedicated to getting prices on products as low as possible for you, me, and hundreds of millions of other people. You and I benefit from their commitment. We get great deals on things we need and want.

WalMart gains market share from competitors because we choose to spend our money with them. Who is the winner? We all are, of course, but WalMart is the biggest winner.

WalMart generates an enormous amount of revenue because they serve a large number of customers by offering them significant value. The process isn't too complicated to understand, but it's really hard to do. The point is that when you focus on serving everyone like a customer, you can become extremely rich.

The richest companies in the world have all found a way to democratize offerings in order to achieve critical mass. That is, they have learned to offer something of great value to lots of customers.

Companies like Microsoft, Apple, Nike, Disney, McDonald's, Google, and Ford serve large numbers of people, and they make large sums of money by doing it. The history of Ford is worth discussing to illustrate the point of serving everyone like a customer. Back in its heyday, Ford was *the* company.

Ford was founded by, surprise, a guy by the name of Henry Ford, who is regarded as the father of the modern assembly line used in mass production[19]. His introduction of the Model T revolutionized transportation and American industry.

The Model T was introduced on October 1, 1908 for—get this—$825! The car was simple to drive and more importantly,

---

[19] (Henry Ford, n.d.)

easy and inexpensive to repair. It was so cheap that by the 1920s, a majority of American motorists learned to drive on the Model T.

Ford served everyone, including his employees. He astonished the world in 1914 by offering a $5-per-day wage, which more than doubled the pay rate of most of his workers. Wall Street criticized Ford for raising the pay of workers because of its potential to reduce profits. The move, however, proved extremely profitable.

Instead of constant employee turnover, the best mechanics flocked to Ford, bringing knowledge and expertise, raising productivity, and lowering costs. Additionally, he proved that paying people more would enable workers to buy the cars they built and would therefore be good for business.

By 1918, half of all cars in America were Model T's. Ford Motor Company had become an industrial juggernaut because he turned everyone into a customer. That was Ford's Fortune of Good Customer Service.

Unfortunately, a puzzling thing happened to Ford that happens to a great many companies and people over time. They forget the customer. Somehow the company started to focus more on itself and how it wanted to do things rather than serve the customer.

As Ford wrote in his autobiography, "Any customer can have a car painted any color that he wants so long as it is black[20]." By the mid-1920s, sales of the Model T began to decline because of rising competition. Why? Other automakers offered payment plans that consumers could use to buy their product. These other cars usually cost more and included more modern mechanical features and styling not available with the Model T, including a choice of various colors. Despite urgings from his son, Ford steadfastly

---

[20] (Ford)

refused to incorporate new features into the Model T or to offer a customer credit plan.

The Ford Motor Company started to suffer the "Inertia of Success" that all companies and people seem to experience if they aren't careful. *Inertia of Success* means that businesses and people continue what they have been doing because they achieved good results in the past. They are convinced that if they keep doing what they have been doing, somehow things will return to the way they were.

But companies and individuals can't keep depending on old ways. They can't expect to offer the same services, while refusing to change but expecting different results. Case in point: No matter how hard a company tries, it cannot get me to go back to using compact discs!

Albert Einstein said, "The definition of insanity is doing the same thing over and over again and expecting different results." The only way to cure the insanity of the inertia is to apply an external force to change the velocity and/or direction of the old way of doing things. The best force to counteract the Inertia of Success comes from the customer. Let customers tell you what they want, and then do it!

Individuals

If I asked you to give a name of someone who is rich, you might say Bill Gates or Warren Buffet. Or you might name a celebrity such as Oprah Winfrey because Oprah runs the world, according to my wife.

How did all these people get rich? Let's figure it out.

We know that Gates is in charge of Microsoft, or used to be, and made a fortune selling Windows, which is an operating system that most of us use on our computer.

He was kind enough to figure out how to help us navigate the computer with his Windows product, and we all thanked him by sending him our money to make him one of the richest men in the world. Not a bad day's work.

Warren Buffett, well, he sits in front of the computer, analyzing stocks, and buys and trades them. Right?

Wrong. Buffett invests money in companies, often buying the entire company, which then serves customers. So in a way, Buffett is like the Wizard of Oz, granting little wishes to lots of people. These people in turn give his companies money, which he in turn gives to his shareholders, who in turn pay his salary. Last I checked he lived pretty close to Kansas, so I'm right about the Wizard of Oz thing, more or less. Or maybe he's the Oracle of Omaha. Same difference.

My point is that we all see how the system of serving everyone like a customer helped Gates and Buffett. You can use the system to achieve the same results.

Whether you're a CEO of a large company or you're trying to figure out how to become the CEO of a large company, you can and will succeed when you learn to serve everyone like a customer. Start by shifting your focus to the needs of your customers. In the process, you will discover a variety of ideas that will make their life better. This will lead you to new ways to build your business or help you start your own business offering new services or products. Either way, you'll improve your fortune when you stop thinking about money and start thinking about customers.

Chapter 3

The Mother Teresa Effect

You might have thought this book would show you only how to get financially rich. Yet serving everyone like a customer will do as much for your health as it will for your wealth. But to make this happen, we have to deprogram your brain because for years, you have heard a bunch of baloney about what it takes to be successful. We have to erase your mental hard drive because you have downloaded philosophical spam that is crippling you.

Much of the philosophical spam you have downloaded to your brain is either driving you mad or holding you back. For instance, many of us have been told that only the strong survive, and that to make it to the top you have to have a take-no-prisoners attitude. After all, it's a dog-eat-dog world, and we all know that nice guys finish last. Right?

Sayings like the ones above do more harm than good. If we let such ideas take root, they will form beliefs that will then govern our behavior or our ideas about what it takes to be successful. Most people don't want to become a super jerk to become a super success, so they never really go for it in life. If they do, they either sabotage themselves halfway through the journey or they become the jerk they thought they needed to become. Funny thing is, the jerks who make it to the top have a hard time staying there. More importantly, you'll learn that if you ride people hard, it might cost you your health. At least that's what I learned one cold morning.

The Type A Personality

It was a January morning in 2009 (and twenty-four degrees below zero, I might add) when I walked out the front door of my house to pick up my copy of the *Wall Street Journal* on the driveway. I got the paper, ran back inside, and pulled the protective plastic bag off.

When I opened the paper, I noticed a picture of Steve Jobs, CEO of Apple Computer, with his head bowed and fist up to his mouth as if to hold back serious emotion. The headline over the picture read, "Apple's Jobs Takes Medical Leave[21]." I was immediately filled with compassion because I guessed the situation was dire.

Jobs had undergone surgery some years before to deal with pancreatic cancer. I wondered if he'd had a relapse. Fortunately,

---

21 (Kane, 2009)

the article quoted a person close to the situation who made it clear that the medical leave was necessary to treat a hormone imbalance. But the article got me thinking about the life and success of Steve Jobs.

Many of us own an iPod, download music from iTunes, use the MacBook, make calls with the iPhone, and organize our life with the iPad, all because of Steve Jobs.

He sure knows how to serve everyone like a customer, I thought, and he has grown rich by doing that.

Steve Jobs was a classic type A personality. Type A's are ambitious, impatient, controlling, and aggressive. They are often brilliant, and they get things done. That's the positive side of the Type A.

The negative side of a type A personality is oftentimes an insensitivity towards people. They may even trample others in pursuit of their goals—something I'm guilty of at times.

It turns out that failing to serve everyone like a customer has an effect on your health. As I was doing some research on the health costs of failing to serve everyone like a customer, I was fortunate to find some startling research about the health costs of being a Type A.

Researchers from Mount Zion Medical Center studied the classic Type A personality, who often copes with life's stress by becoming hostile, angry, and aggressive toward other people. They discovered that these people were more likely to experience higher levels of cholesterol, triglycerides, and catecholamine, all of which increase the risk of coronary disease[22].

When I discovered the health costs of a type A personality, I was alarmed. I decided to broaden and deepen my research.

---

[22] (Luks & Payne, 1991, 2001)

I discovered another study of thirteen thousand people where researchers found that those who exhibited type A characteristics were almost three times as likely to have a heart attack[23].

Why?

When you feel hostile, angry, or stressed out, your sympathetic nervous system (governed by the hypothalamus) sends a hormone, corticotropin-releasing factor (CRF), to your pituitary gland. This in turn, sends a hormone called adrenocorticotropin (ACTH) through the bloodstream to the adrenal glands. As a result, the adrenal glands release certain hormones like cortisol and catecholamine into your bloodstream[24].

Notable effects of catecholamine include increased heart rate and blood pressure, blood vessel constriction in the skin and gastrointestinal tract, blood vessel dilation in skeletal muscles, bronchiole dilation in the lungs, and decreased metabolism. These are all characteristics of the fight-or-flight response[25,26]. That response is valuable in times of serious danger or stress when you need to have heightened senses, but overexposure to the hormones that cause such a response can have long-term consequences far more dangerous than you probably realize.

Higher levels of catecholamine in the blood for prolonged periods will increase the risk of coronary disease, as well as cholesterol. It might also contribute to weight problems because it lowers your metabolism.

Cortisol, on the other hand, increases the glucose in the blood[27]. If elevated levels of cortisol remain in the system, it can lead to hyperglycemia, which can result in diabetes. High levels

---

[23] (Griffin, n.d.)

[24] (Stress Related Illinesses, n.d.)

[25] (Adrenal Medulla, n.d.)

[26] (Catecholamine, n.d.)

[27] (Cortisol, n.d.)

of cortisol can also weaken the immune system which in turn, prevents the proliferation of T cells, a specific type of white blood cell that fights infections and cancer[28]. Cortisol also lowers bone formation and as a consequence may engender osteoporosis. Moreover, long-term exposure to cortisol will result in damage to the hippocampus of your brain, resulting in a decreased ability to learn.

That's not all. Anger and depression may be linked to these conditions[29]. Moreover, depression seems to cause the same problems as anger. This makes sense since depression can be thought of as anger directed toward oneself. More importantly, anger directed at yourself or others causes significant health problems.

For instance, it appears that depression also raises the level of cortisol in the body, which has a number of consequences in addition to those already noted. One such consequence is that it inhibits the absorption of insulin. As might be expected, ten percent of diabetic men and twenty percent of diabetic women are also clinically depressed[30]. Other studies have shown that the depressed are also likely to experience reduced appetite, suffer from ulcers, and become more susceptible to pathogens[31].

The number of top-selling prescription drugs used to treat many if not all effects of anger and depression suggests that many people are, well, angry, depressed, and overstressed (see table below).

---

28 (cancer.gov, n.d.)

29 (Koh, Kim, Kim, & Park, 2005)

30 (mindpub.com, n.d.)

31 (Luks & Payne, 1991, 2001)

Top-Selling Prescription Drugs[32]

Rank	Brand Name	2010 Sales ($ bn)	Medical Use
1	Lipitor®	$7.2	Cholesterol
2	Nexium®	$6.3	Gastrointestinal Disorders
3	Plavix®	$6.1	Thrombotic Events
4	Advair Diskus®	$4.7	Asthma
5	Abilify®	$4.6	Antidepressant
6	Seroquel®	$4.4	Antidepressant
7	Singulair®	$4.1	Asthma
8	Crestor®	$3.8	Cholesterol
9	Actos®	$3.5	Diabetes
10	Epogen®	$3.3	Kidney Disease

A study conducted by the American Psychological Association in 2008 found that sixty percent of people get irritable or angry because of stress. Even more revealing is that seventy-five to ninety percent of all doctor's office visits are stress-related, and forty-three percent of adults suffer adverse health effects from stress[33]. As you might expect, health-care expenditures are about fifty percent higher for highly stressed employees than for other employees, according to the *Journal of Occupational and Environmental Medicine*[34].

If you are a business leader managing a large team, you should consider that about thirty cents of every dollar you make goes to deal with health issues. Also, and the number-one driver

[32] (Herper, 2011)
[33] (healthywomen.com, n.d.)
[34] (pacificsource.com, n.d.)

of those costs may in fact be your angry, stressed-out employees. It pays to figure out how to manage this growing problem[35].

The Mother Teresa Effect

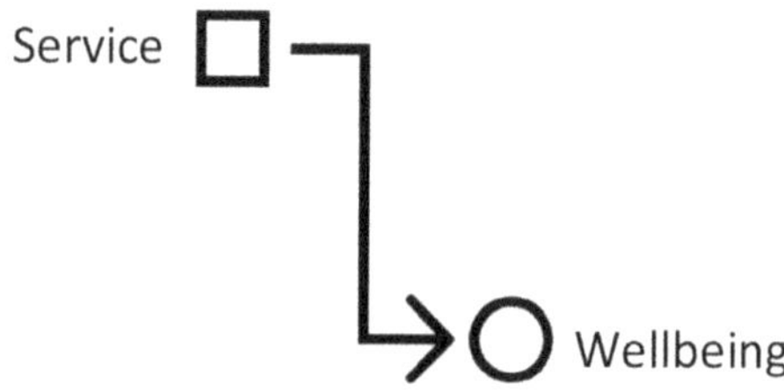

There is no question that being hard on people will rob you of good health. Letting others get to you will also affect you poorly and may lead to depression and other ills.

Most causes of anger and depression stem from our perception of people and of ourselves. We get angry when we think that other people aren't behaving according to plan. We get depressed when we convince ourselves we aren't any good. Neither view is the right perspective because the focus is on you instead of the customer. You'll lose your wealth and your health when you take your focus off the customer.

As soon as you change your focus and serve everyone like a customer by finding ways to truly help them, you will see measurable effects on your health.

As surprising as this may sound, just observing heartfelt acts of service can improve your immune system.

Researchers at Harvard Medical School took samples of saliva from 132 students before and after they watched a moving fifty-minute documentary. The film showcased Mother Teresa's

---

35 (Luks & Payne, 1991, 2001)

efforts to help the sick and dying people of Calcutta, India. The researchers tested the students' saliva to measure the level of immunoglobulin-A (S-IgA), which is a critical defense against cold viruses. They discovered that the level of S-IgA increased dramatically after students watched the film. This has become known as the "Mother Teresa Effect."

Some might find it amazing to know that simply watching a film of people helping people (serving everyone like a customer) can strengthen the immune system. Even more amazing is that there is anecdotal evidence that simply remembering acts of service and kindness to others can likewise increase the S-IgA.

I want you to try the Mother Teresa experiment, although I'm not going to make you spit in a glass, and you don't have to go anywhere. Instead, all I want you to do is watch a video online and observe how you feel. This will be fun, I promise.

Sit down at your computer, open an Internet browser, and go to Youtube.com. When you get to the site, search for a video by Liberty Mutual named "Half Acre." You can do this by going up to the Search box at the top of the page and then typing in "Liberty Mutual ad (1st edition): Half Acre." Click on the first video option that matches the name and watch it. Note how you feel and then come back to the book so we can discuss. You may want to watch it a second or third time to make sure you got the gist of the video.

Now that you have seen the video (at least I hope you have), I want you to think about how it made you feel. Did you feel warmth all over your body when you viewed it?

Did you get chills? If you did, you likely benefited from the Mother Teresa Effect in your body and felt the "Helper's High." You now know what it feels like to serve everyone like a customer.

You can feel that way every day and, in the process, build a better world and become prosperous while doing it. But you have to choose to make it a reality.

So, *"What's your policy?"*

The Helper's High

In their book *The Healing Power of Doing Good,* Allan Luks and Peggy Payne report the results of a survey of three thousand volunteers.

Nine out of ten reported a physical sensation as a result of helping other people, much like you probably did when you watched "Half Acre." Of these, fifty-four percent mentioned a feeling of warmth, twenty-nine percent cited increased levels of energy, and twenty-one percent reported a drug like euphoria. The term Helper's High has been used to describe these feelings people report when helping other people.

The warmth that volunteers reported is related to increased blood flow to the muscles in the arms and legs and a simultaneous contraction of the peripheral blood vessels.

The reverse happens when you are under stress and may explain why you might have cold hands at times.

The authors point out that the increase in energy reported by the volunteers is likely due to the fact that they have reduced the hypermetabolic state caused by stress. Which in turn reduced the body's consumption of oxygen, decreased the heart rate, lowered the blood pressure, and caused the muscles to relax. But the Helper's High itself is likely the result of endorphins' being released into the body.

The pituitary gland and the hypothalamus produce endorphins during times of intense physical exercise. This physiological response to exercise has become known as the "runners high," named by the runners who have reported it. Endorphins resemble opiates in their ability to produce analgesia and a deep sense of well-being. Thus, they are like natural pain relievers and feel-good drugs. This might explain the feeling that helpers get when they volunteer to do helpful things, genuinely giving of themselves without an expectation of getting anything in return.

The Benefits

Evidence suggests that those who serve everyone like a customer are growing rich in health. In particular, the research is based on those who volunteer. Volunteering is perhaps the best example of serving everyone like a customer. A lot of research shows that volunteers have better health than those who don't.

When the University of Michigan studied 1,211 seniors for seven years, researchers discovered that people who volunteered at least forty hours in a year lived longer compared to nonvolunteers[36].

---

36 (htt3)

Another study of 2,700 men tracked their physical health and social activities for ten years and found that those who volunteered regularly had death rates two and a half times lower than those who didn't[37].

Additionally, researchers at Harvard Medical School have concluded that when we develop "a connection of deep affiliation," we trigger emotions that seem to affect the immune system. The researchers discovered that people who had a high level of affiliative trust (perhaps best defined as a belief in the inherent goodness of people) had a greater ratio of helper-to-suppressor T-cells, which indicates that these people are better able to fight disease and infection.

Long-term studies have shown that those people with high affiliative trust showed fewer instances of major illness[38].

Helping others can increase longevity and may even help combat many diseases and conditions. Some of the evidence is anecdotal, and some is direct, but the benefits to your health are indisputable. Let's review a few of the ways that service may help your health.

Weight Control

As noted previously, when you are angry and stressed, your metabolism slows. This will cause you to reach for comfort foods

[37] (Thor, 2006)

[38] (Childers & Grauds, 2005)

as a coping mechanism. By serving everyone like a customer, you will return your metabolism to normal levels, which will help you burn calories and lose weight. Furthermore, if you shift your focus to something besides food, namely other people, that will help you reduce your intake.

Cancer

Research suggests that you might be able to control the level of natural killer (NK) cells by serving others. For instance, the white blood cells that attack cancer cells declined in strength in people who were lonely[39]. By serving everyone like a customer, you may find you'll have many friends and are never alone.

Heart Disease

Heart disease is an epidemic. It is the number-one killer of Americans today, causing seven hundred thousand deaths every year. Research shows that reducing hostility can lower the risk of

[39] (Luks & Payne, 1991, 2001)

a heart attack and will reduce the chance of having another one. Also, those who have more friends have less-constricted coronary arteries than those who are more isolated[40]. Even more interesting is that a key factor in heart disease may be related to the degree that you are self-centered. Research has shown a strong correlation between a person's self-references and focus on I/me and his blood pressure levels.

Researchers at Duke University developed suggestions for counteracting some of the psychosocial risk factors of heart disease. One recommendation was to "put yourself in another person's shoes." Other studies have found that consideration and love for others, manifested in behaviors that reduce hostility, reduce subsequent heart attacks by fifty percent.

All these studies and observations strongly suggest that The Hidden Fortune of Service is also great health.

[40] (Luks & Payne, 1991, 2001)

Chapter 4

The Do-Good, Feel-Good Phenomenon

We experience life through our emotions. If we feel great, life is wonderful. If we feel bad, life is awful.

People will go to great lengths to escape emotional pain by finding ways to cope (e.g. food, drugs, sex, and even death). Emotional needs of people in your life are often more important than physical needs.

Many years ago, a psychologist conducted an experiment using baby monkeys to determine the importance of emotional needs versus physical needs. The subjects were divided into two groups, with each group having two inanimate monkey avatars in their cage.

In the first group, one of the avatars was made of wire and had a bottle filled with milk attached to it. The second monkey avatar did not have a bottle but was made of terrycloth to imitate the fur and warmth of the real mother monkey.

In the second group, one of the avatars was made of wire but did not have a bottle. The second avatar had a bottle and was also made of terrycloth.

Wire and Cloth Monkey Avatars[41]

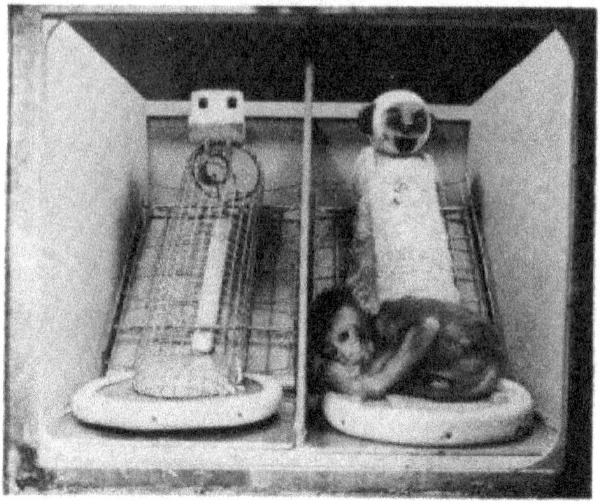

The scientist introduced half the baby monkeys to one of the two groups to see which avatar the baby monkeys would choose. In both groups the baby monkeys selected the warmth of the terrycloth monkey avatar, whether or not that avatar had a bottle of milk. This suggests that emotional needs were by far more important than the physical need for food[42].

Emotional needs are just as critical for people. Several research studies at the turn of the twentieth century investigated the response of babies who lacked emotional nurturing and physical touch. The result was death in over fifty percent of the cases, even though these babies received adequate food and medical care[43]. The phenomenon is called "failure to thrive."

41 (Harlow, 1958)

42 (Harry Harlow, n.d.)

43 (Save the babies: American public health reform and the prevention of infant mortality, 1850–1929 , n.d.)

If you do not serve the emotional needs of your customers, they may fail to thrive, and you may also. People need the positive emotional reassurance of those around them to do well.

Many people quietly walk a path of sorrows. We often don't know all they've been through or where they're coming from. We know only what we see, which is often distorted because many of us have learned to put on a happy face. We lie with our smiles because we don't want to be a burden. It's a real shame because people need people to help them with things that were caused by other people.

Most of the pain we feel comes from how others have treated us. Suffering the scoffs, scorn, name-calling, prejudice, rejection, and hatred of others takes a tremendous toll on the victim. Only recently have we begun to understand the magnitude of that toll.

Consider the emotional impact on a person who is ostracized or rejected. Scientists have used magnetic resonance imaging (MRI) to determine where various emotions, including the feeling of rejection, register in the brain. They found that when people feel ostracized, the anterior cingulate cortex activates, which is the same place in the brain that registers physical pain[44].

Think about that for a minute.

When a person is ostracized, ridiculed, or hated, their emotional response feels just like physical pain. How many people are walking around feeling hurt without us knowing it? It's why Black Lives Matter. It's why All Lives Matter.

Rejection or stress can alter cognitive abilities, lessening the capacity to learn, solve problems, or even innovate. Think about the business impact of a group of employees who feel rejected or overly stressed.

---

[44] Goleman, 2006, 2007)

Such a situation could rob a business of real opportunities to innovate products or grow sales. It could also create significant health problems, increasing health-care costs, decreasing productivity, and increasing employee turnover.

None of these things are good for business; yet, we still shove people into office cubicles like cow stalls, where they are milked for all of their ideas, energy, and work products.

Eventually, these cow people are put out to pasture or just shot—I mean fired—when they aren't producing enough. But if we woke up and realized that we can get more out of employees by serving them like customers, then maybe we'd be able to transform the workplace into something enjoyable, efficient, and highly productive.

Research has shown that the way managers treat their employees not only influences job satisfaction but it can also raise or lower employee blood pressure[45]. Therefore, the boss can have a significant impact on the well-being of those s/he manages. The right working conditions can increase job satisfaction, improve morale and health, and encourage risk-taking to launch new products, which is tantamount to entrepreneurship.

Consider companies such as Bain, Chick-Fil-A, Facebook, Google, HEB, Microsoft, Salesfoce.com, Southwest Airlines, and T-Mobile who have extremely high employee ratings as reported by Glassdoor.com[46]. These companies go out of their way to treat people well and compensate them fairly. Consequently, these companies have amongst the highest revenue and earnings growth rates within their peer class.

You can improve your fortune by developing a deep concern for the well-being of others and then acting on that concern

---

45 (Goleman, 2006, 2007)

46 (Best Places to Work 2020, n.d.)

through service. Doing that often starts by learning to love other people, including your customers and employees.

Love is an immensely important need for people. We all want it. Babies can even die without it. Love is so powerful that it can even alleviate pain. The most curious aspect of love is that the more love you give, the more love you get.

Science has shown that when you truly love somebody, the brain activates neurotransmitters that create a burst of pleasure for both the giver and the receiver[47]. This means you can feel love by simply giving love. The more love you give, the richer in love you become.

Some interesting studies of nurses demonstrate the impact of their compassion on patient health. When nurses were loving and caring, both the patients and the nurses felt better. Positive, caring acts do as much if not more for us than for our customers.

This is the great relationship paradox, and it is the secret to emotional strength and enduring relationships. This is the do-good feel-good phenomenon.

The best way to get love is to give love. If you take this approach, you will feel love simply by giving it to someone, whether that person reciprocates or not. What's more, people will feel compelled to love you back if you love them first. If you continue to love your customers unconditionally over some period of time, your mere presence will cause their brain to release oxytocin into their bloodstream, which creates good feelings.

When you've conditioned people to have a positive response to your presence, you become like a drug. They will keep coming back for more. You might have to turn away business because you can't handle the demand!

---

47 (Goleman, 2006, 2007)

Chapter 5

The Reciprocity Norm

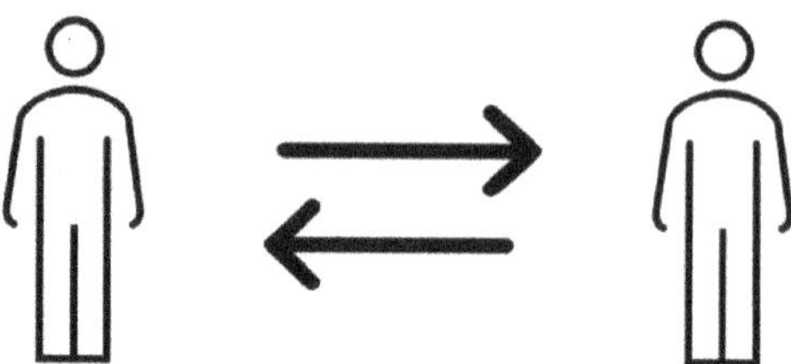

When somebody does something for you, you may have a desire to return the favor. In some instances, they may even expect you to return the favor. In social psychology we call this "The Reciprocity Norm."

According to researchers, the obligation to repay others or reciprocate what they do for you appears to be culturally universal[48]. The social obligation of exchanging a give for every take is well documented[49]. In other words, when someone gives you something of perceived value, you immediately respond with the desire to give something back. To some degree, reciprocity controls all of us.

Think about your experience in restaurants. Do you normally tip your server? I sure hope so, but if you're like most of us, you will feel obligated to do so. Why? Because we have been raised to

48 (Diekmann, n.d.)

49 (Million & Lerner, n.d.)

believe that tipping the waitstaff fifteen to twenty percent of the tab honors their service to us.

The Reciprocity Norm works in all areas of our life. Consider something as simple as a sneeze. When you sneeze and someone near you says, “Bless you,” what do you do? You say, “Thank you.” Also, if I smile at you and say hello, chances are you will do the same. And the list goes on.

The Reciprocity Norm is so strong that even when gifts and favors are unsolicited (or unwanted), the recipient feels compelled to give something in return.

Two researchers proved that point when they mailed Christmas cards to a sample of complete strangers. To their surprise, about twenty percent responded by sending holiday greeting cards to the return address[50]!

Other researchers ran an experiment in which they created a two-person game to test the reciprocity norm. To start, Player A got $10. If that player kept the money, Player *B* also got $10, and the game ended. But if Player A chose to let Player *B* take a turn, then Player *B* faced a choice: take home $40 and leave nothing for Player A, or take $25 and leave $15 for player A.

The Reciprocity Game

---

50 (The Psychology of Safety Handbook, n.d.)

About half the time, Player A chose to let Player *B* into the game, forgoing a sure $10. In response, nearly three-quarters of the Player *Bs* decided to split the $40 with player A[51]. What does that tell you? If you serve everyone like a customer, you can bet that most (maybe seventy-five percent) will respond positively. The Reciprocity Norm is so strong that people can be influenced to do almost anything.

Nonprofit charities and other companies use this principle all the time to get people to donate money. They send out free address labels, key rings, or other freebies, hoping to get a donation. And guess what? It works.

If you are not employing The Reciprocity Norm with your customers or coworkers, then you can't expect them to do anything for you. You should always find ways to give something of value with no expectation of return. When you do this you demonstrate that you are sincere, and you build good will. More often than not, you will find that people go out of their way to return the favor.

A Really Big Tip

On December 30, 2007, *USA Today* reported a story about a waitress, a dead customer, $50,000, and a car. What do these things have in common? Meet Melina Salazar.

For many years Melina worked at Luby's Cafeteria in Brownsville, Texas. She always did her best to serve her customers. Like most waitresses, she had her share of obnoxious customers whom she no doubt wished to go away. But she will never forget one of her toughest customers.

For almost seven years Melina did her best to satisfy every need of her most cantankerous but loyal customer, a man named Walter "Buck" Swords. Melina made sure that Buck's food was as hot as he

[51] (htt4)

wanted, even if it meant he burned his mouth. She smiled despite his demands and his curses. But rarely are things as they seem.

Buck was an industrious guy, having owned and operated his own trucking company for forty years[52]. He stood at about five feet, nine inches, weighed 180 pounds, and wore two very big diamond rings on his hand. Buck would tell others that he didn't really like to wear the diamonds, but he inherited them from his late brother. No doubt he wore the diamonds as a reminder of loved ones past. He was a lonely man just trying to hold on to a sense of family and belonging.

Buck died in July 2007 in Brownsville, Texas. He had no immediate family to grieve for him. But before he left this world he had decided to leave Melina $50,000 and a 2000 Buick—a gesture of gratitude for her kindness and compassion.

To Buck, Melina was family. She probably had no idea what her kindness meant to him.

Melina learned just a few days before Christmas 2007 that Buck had left her the money and car[53]. "I still can't believe it," she told Harlingen television station KGBT-TV in an interview, during which she described Buck as "kind of mean."

You might be wondering if I think you should accept hurtful treatment as Melina did and serve everyone like a customer, no matter what. Here is my really big tip: Serve *everyone* like a customer.

What do you gain if you're picky about whom you serve? Should you save your best smile only for people who are nice to you? Do you really gain much when you are selective with whom you give your best? The answer is no.

If you serve only those who are nice to you, you might find that you don't have many people to serve at all. Is that good business? Think about it.

---

52 (htt5)

53 (Waitress Gets $50,000 From Cranky Customer, n.d.)

Melina discovered The Hidden Fortune of Service by serving everyone like a customer—good or bad. In the end her service paid off. If you serve everyone like a customer, good things will happen to you and your company. That's a fact.

A Really Big Fortune Cookie

Your fortune will change when you serve everyone like a customer.

On Friday, December 7, 2007, the Associated Press reported a story about a woman whose bequest shocked her heirs and the British courts.

Golda Bechal was a wealthy and lonely widow who frequently visited a Chinese restaurant northeast of London. The owners, Kim Sing Man and his wife, Bee Lian, had been kind to Golda. They prepared her food just the way she liked it. They talked to her and showed her kindness. They loved her.

Golda died in 1994 at the age of eighty-eight. In her will, she said that she wanted Kim Sing Man and his wife to inherit her money in order to repay them for their kindness in what were the golden years of her life.

She left them $21 million.

Golda's five nephews and nieces went to court to have the will declared invalid, claiming that their aunt was suffering from dementia. They asked the judge to give the inheritance to them. But the High Court judge ruled that the will was legal.

Judge Donald Rattee accepted the restaurateurs' evidence that Golda, sad and lonely after the death of her husband and son, became like a family member to the couple.

Golda had gone on foreign holidays with Kim and his wife and regularly got together with them at their restaurant and at her apartment in Mayfair, central London.

"It was not irrational to leave the bulk of her estate to Mrs. Man, the daughter she would dearly wished to have had," Rattee said[54]. The reciprocity norm compelled Golda to leave her wealth to Kim and his wife because they had given Golda the best service possible. They sincerely cared about her and served her the best they could.

Perhaps Golda's will is the biggest fortune cookie message of all: Serve everyone like a customer if you want to become wealthy, healthy and happy.

You Are My Customer

Let's think about you for a minute since you are my primary customer here. Perhaps you picked up this book with the goal of

[54] (CBS News, 2007)

becoming more successful. Perhaps someone gave it to you, or maybe you found it lying around somewhere and picked it up to see what it was about. Regardless of how you acquired this book, it is in your hands now.

Think of this book as an opportunity to try something new to improve your chances of achieving success. The strategies presented here have been proven to work. By the time you're done reading it, you will find that your career and business prospects will change for the better to some degree if you apply the principles and information you learn.

For those of you who so desire, your prospects will change dramatically. But it's up to you to decide just how much you want your life to change. The choice is—and has always been—yours to make.

If you want more money, you will find it. If you want to invent a new service, you will do it. If you want a promotion, you will get it. You can have any of these things and more if you change you as the product and learn to serve everyone like a customer.

Henry Ford once said, "Whether you think that you can or that you can't, you are usually right." His point is that the outcomes in your life are up to you. You can make it big, if that's what you want, or you can lose it big, if that's what you want.

You might think I'm a little crazy to say that some people sabotage themselves, but it happens all the time. One rude comment to the wrong person can destroy a career or a business opportunity. Failing to serve your employer as your customer could cost you your job.

If you have already lost some important business opportunities because of poor service, you may think you're finished. Let me say to you that all of that is baloney. You can turn any situation around by providing extraordinary service. Start by leveraging The Reciprocity Norm, and you can get people to start giving back.

Chapter 6

The Waiter Rule

You have probably heard the phrase, "*The customer is always right*[55]." Harry Gordon Selfridge coined that term, or so some think.

Selfridge was a driven man who worked his way up the ranks at Marshall Field's department stores, married into a prominent family, and amassed enough money to found the Selfridge's chain of department stores in the United Kingdom[56]. Some believe that Selfridge may have gotten the expression "the customer is always right" from Marshall Field. Regardless of who coined the phrase, it has become a common albeit antiquated term about how to serve customers.

I find it amusing that somebody by the name of *Selfridge* (self-emphasized) would be associated with what seems to be a *selfless* concept—a little bit of irony, no doubt. However, Selfridge's philosophy was anything but selfless. He wanted to make money.

---

55 (htt6)

56 (Selfridges, n.d.)

Perhaps one of Selfridge's best innovations was making shopping a fun adventure instead of a chore. He put merchandise on display so customers could examine it, and he put the highly profitable perfume counter front-and-center on the ground floor. He also established policies that made shopping safe and easy—techniques adopted by modern department stores the world over.

Selfridge set up educational and scientific exhibits in his stores. He himself was interested in education and science and believed that the displays would introduce potential new customers to Selfridge's, generating both immediate and long-term sales.

In 1909, Selfridge exhibited the airplane used in the first cross-channel flight, where it was seen by twelve thousand people[57]. One could argue that such displays had little direct relationship to the bottom line. Yet, by giving his customers something of value for free, he received free publicity, generated store traffic, gained new customers, and increased revenues.

I think Selfridge was convinced that to do well and thrive in business, he needed to *serve everyone like a customer.* The strategy worked.

I have said before that everyone is a customer, but you probably think that contradicts the definition of *customer.* But what is the exact definition of a customer?

> "cust•tom•er [pronounced kuhs-tuh-mer] – noun 1. A person who purchases goods or services from another; buyer; patron. 2. Informal. A person one has to deal with: a tough customer; a cool customer[58]."

---

[57] (Selfridges, n.d.)

[58] (Customer, n.d.)

You probably guessed the first definition. But based on the informal definition above, a customer can also be "a person one has to deal with." That's a pretty broad definition and possibly a surprise to you. This sense of the word includes such people as your family, your coworkers, your boss, your clients, your teacher, your teenaged kids (yikes!), and even a cab driver.

Why? They are all people you have to deal with, and therefore they fit the informal definition.

Perhaps that seems extreme. You might think that people such as your teacher or a cab driver are not customers. I beg to differ. If you serve everyone like a customer, including people such as teachers and cab drivers, you will find favor with these people. What I mean is that you will get preferred service and support. You will find that most of the time these people will go out of their way to help you if you serve them like a customer instead of someone who is beneath you. And you never know who might be watching how you treat people.

The Waiter Rule

Have you ever heard of the "Waiter Rule"? I'd like to share a little story that will illustrate a very important rule of leadership and its resulting Fortune. Let me introduce you to Stan Cool.

Stan Cool is a business executive who is on his way to interview for a new position with an industrial manufacturer in

Atlanta, Georgia. Stan had just gotten into a cab at the Atlanta airport when he looked down at his Rolex watch and noticed that he was running late.

Stan said to the cab driver, "Look, I really don't care how you do it, but I need you to move your ass and get me to 222 Liberty Street." The cab driver, made nervous by the brashness of his customer's tone, sat up in his seat, gripped the steering wheel, and pressed the gas pedal. As the driver made an obvious attempt to hurry, Stan mumbled under his breath a derogatory comment about the cab driver's ethnicity.

When the cab reached the destination, Stan looked at the meter and threw his money onto the front seat, leaving the driver a one-dollar tip for a $40 fare. As the driver gathered up the cash, Stan got out of the cab, slammed the door, and looked up at the hotel to find the address. That's when he realized it was the wrong place.

By now the cab driver had left, and Stan was lost, with only five minutes left before his interview.

A few people walked past Stan, and one of them, an old man, smiled at him, but Stan didn't respond.

Curious, the man decided to stop and watch Stan because he looked boiling mad and ready to attack. Stan raced around the valet area, trying to find someone who could tell him how to get to his interview.

"Hey, you! Where is 222 Liberty Street?" Stan snapped at a young doorman coming out of the lobby.

"Well that's just right around the corner, sir. Of course, you can always just come in through the lobby if you like." The doorman said.

"What? Is this the place?" Stan asked.

"Yes, sir. The address you gave me is for the front of the hotel. You're on the backside," the door man replied.

"Why didn't you just say that? I'm late for an important meeting, and I'm a guest here!" Stan fired back.

"I'm sorry, sir," the doorman replied. "I was just trying to answer your question."

"What's your name?" Stan demanded as he squinted at the doorman's name badge.

The doorman said, "Tyrone, sir."

"I'll deal with you when I come back," Stan told him. He marched toward the lobby, shooting angry glances back at Tyrone.

When Stan entered the hotel lounge, he pointed at a young hostess.

"I'm supposed to meet somebody by the name of Gerald St. Claire. Do you know where he's sitting?"

"He hasn't arrived yet, sir. Would you like me to seat you?" The hostess replied.

Stan said yes.

While he was following the hostess to the table, the old man Stan had ignored outside crept into the hotel to witness Stan and all of the ruckus he was making. After Stan sat down, he noticed the old man glaring at him. Stan got irritated at the man, grimaced at him, and then turned away to speak to the waitress who had just stepped up.

"Hello, sir. Welcome to the Executive Lounge. Can I get you something to drink?"

"I'll have a Pellegrino," he said, then sat back in his chair and picked up the newspaper that lay neatly folded in front of him.

"I'll get that for you right away," the waitress replied, smiled, then walked away.

The old man who had smiled at Stan outside, even more curious now, walked into the lounge and slowly approached Stan's table.

The old man looked as if he was on vacation or perhaps returning from a golf course because he looked a bit disheveled.

The old man approached Stan and said, "I couldn't help but notice you. It looks like you're having a bad day."

"It's been ridiculous. If there were more competent people in the world, I wouldn't have these problems." Stan replied.

That's when the old man said, "My name is Gerald St. Claire. I'm guessing you're Stan Cool."

At this point Stan was noticeably shaken as he remembered that he hadn't acknowledged Mr. St. Claire when he got out of the cab. Stan stood up immediately and said, "Mr. St. Claire! It's a pleasure to meet you. Please sit down."

As Mr. St Claire pulled out a chair to sit down, Stan's bag fell over, and the returning waitress tripped on it, causing the Pellegrino to spill all over Stan's bag. The waitress was stunned, then horrified, and finally was profusely apologetic as she quickly tried to dry off Stan's bag.

"Incompetent. Absolutely incompetent," Stan said as he walked around the table and quickly dismissed the waitress. Mr. St. Claire just watched this little drama with a careful eye as Stan shooed the waitress away.

"I'm sorry, Mr. St. Claire," Stan said. "It's been one thing after another today."

"No, no, no," Mr. St. Claire replied. "It's okay. But all of this reminds me of when I was younger. I was once a waiter myself at a hotel much like this one. That was a long time ago. I remember this one time I was serving a woman a glass of wine, and I somehow dropped the glass, and the red wine spilled all over her beautiful white dress. I was devastated and worried I might lose my job. I felt terrible, but to my surprise the woman touched my arm and said that it was okay and that it was her fault. I'll never forget that woman and the kindness she showed me. You can always tell somebody's true character by how they treat people in a subordinate position. And Stan, you have taught me a lot about you."

Mr. St. Claire stood up, extended his hand to Stan, and said, "It's been a pleasure." Then Mr. St. Claire walked over to the waitress to console her and assure her that what happened was not her fault but his.

The CEO of the Raytheon corporation, Bill Swanson, wrote a book of thirty-three short leadership principles called *Swanson's Unwritten Rules*. Rule 32 states: "A person who is nice to you (the CEO) but rude to the waiter or to others is not a nice person. (This rule never fails)." This is called the Waiter Rule[59].

Swanson says that he developed the waiter rule when he was eating with someone who became "absolutely obnoxious" to a waiter, all because the restaurant didn't carry a certain wine.

"Watch out for people who have a situational value system, who can turn the charm on and off depending on the status of the person they are interacting with," writes Swanson. "Be especially wary of those who are rude to people perceived to be in subordinate roles."

Some years ago *USA Today* interviewed many CEOs, all of whom agreed that the Waiter Rule is true and that it provides the best window into the character of people.

Au Bon Pain cofounder Ron Shaich, who later became the CEO of Panera Bread, agreed. He said he once interviewed someone for a position as general counsel and observed that the person was "sweet" to him but turned "amazingly rude" to a bus boy. Turns out the candidate didn't get the job.

The CEO of Sara Lee, Brenda Barnes, pointed out that by some twist of fate in life, the customer becomes the waiter. Barnes confirmed my own conclusions: everyone is your customer.

---

59 (Swanson's Unwritten Rules, n.d.)

Coincidentally, Ms. Barnes was a waitress in her early career, and in her case, the servant became the master and the master became the servant. It always works that way. Her epiphany is your greatest insight into what it takes to become a super success. Think like a CEO and serve everyone like a customer.

The Waiter Rule is important if only to manage the impressions you make because you never know who is watching.

Take Stan, for instance. If he had known better, he would have realized that Mr. St. Claire was his customer, but he didn't act that way until he knew who Mr. St. Claire was. By that point, it was too late. He exposed his true character and made it clear he didn't have the right stuff to be a leader and care for people.

You can't maintain a dual value system and expect to succeed. If you treat some people as superiors because of who they are and others with disrespect, then you will weaken your ability to serve everyone and spot needs. You can't do things halfway. If you want to achieve success, you have to devote yourself to people completely.

If you serve everyone like a customer, you will find that people will reciprocate your actions. Others will notice that, and you'll invoke The Hidden Fortune of Service.

Chapter 7

Everyone is Your Customer

To realize The Hidden Fortune of Service, you have to do something meaningful and special for your customers. But customers are often as different on the inside as they are on the outside, so you can't expect everybody to want to be treated the same. If we are going to provide excellent service, we should treat customers as they want to be treated by doing something they value and appreciate.

For example, I wouldn't find any value if you gave me a giant stuffed panda bear wearing pink underwear. Besides thinking you might be disturbed (although strangely curious and mildly intriguing), I'd probably avoid you like the plague. Similarly, if you give oddball gifts to your customers, don't be surprised if they shy away from you or worse, even hold you in contempt. You have to serve each customer uniquely.

Most customers you meet can be classified into groups called segments. A segment is usually comprised of people who have needs and wants that are similar to one another and yet unique from everyone else's. The unique needs of a segment are precisely what makes a segment a segment.

So what customer segments do you serve? Do they have children? Are they stay-at-home moms? Are they MILFs? Of course *MILF* stands for "Men in Little Ferraris." What did you think I meant?

The most successful people and companies focus their energies on serving groups of customers that share common characteristics. Tony Hsieh, the CEO of Zappos.com, built a billion-dollar business and became a multimillionaire in the process because he focused on serving the needs of consumers who like to buy shoes online[60]. His customer segment of online shoe buyers is relatively narrow, but it allowed him to focus on providing a superior customer-service experience, which helped him grow a huge business. Hsieh's service strategies have become well studied by other companies and individuals wanting to duplicate his spectacular success.

The more specific you get about whom you serve, the better position you'll be in to achieve The Hidden Fortune of Service.

In general, you'll find seven basic characteristics you can use to identify a segment or group of customers you'd like to serve. We'll discuss each of them, using this diagram:

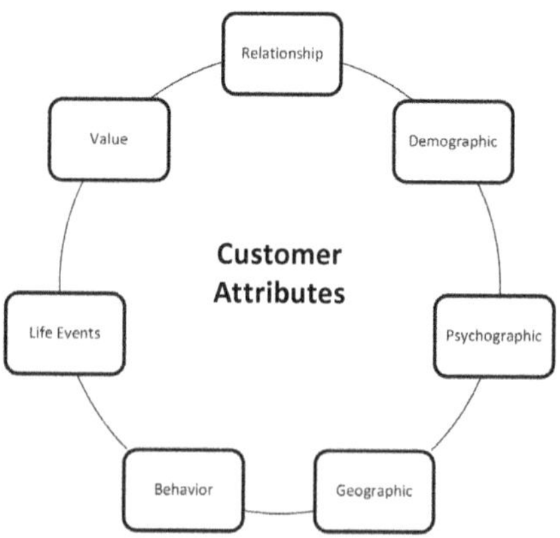

[60] Tony Hsieh, Wikipedia.

Relationships

As a starting point, you can group your customers according to the type of relationship you have with them.

Remember, everyone is your customer, so your relationship doesn't have to be predicated on money. It can be based on anything.

Here are some examples:

- Paying customer
- Coworker customer
- Superior (Boss) customer
- Employee customer
- Shareholder customer
- Supplier customer
- Partner customer
- Classmate customer
- Citizen customer
- Server (like a store clerk) customer
- Family customer

The customer suffix is just a reminder that you serve people in every relationship. I use it to emphasize the point that service should be a core principle in every relationship, albeit in different ways. As an example, you don't want to treat your family customers like your employees. Can you imagine treating your spouse like an employee? Okay, don't answer that.

We all seem to understand that each relationship we have requires a different protocol. That is, we don't give orders to our spouse, and we don't fondle the waiter. At least I hope not.

Customers have expectations about how you should serve them. Those expectations are governed by the relationship type you have with them. Placing your customers in the proper relationship category helps you to know what and how to serve.

In the business world, we marketing people often say that not all customers are created equal. This is because some are worth more than others. That is an awfully blunt way to say that some customers are of more value to the firm, but the point is valid. Because customers are not created equal, you must identify the relationships that are the most important and separate those from the rest. Your most important customers will expect you to give them preferred treatment if you want to keep them.

Demographics

Demographics are usually the external characteristics of a person. Age, gender, race, national origin, income level, marital status, religion, family composition, and the presence of children in the household all qualify as demographic information.

You can group and serve customers based on their demographics. For instance, think of gender. Does it matter? Of course it does. Women account for eighty-three percent of all the money spent in the U.S[61]. That is about $4 trillion of purchasing power annually. Women rule.

[61] ('Men Buy, Women Shop': The Sexes Have Different Priorities When Walking Down the Aisles, 2007)

Customers who make over $100,000 in household income could be another good target[62]. When it comes to food, they spend about seventy-five percent more than the average household. People in this income bracket also spend eighty-two percent more than average on housing and ninety-two percent more than average on transportation.

Demographics can help you identify groups of people to serve. But in order to serve them, you need to understand them inside and out.

Psychographics

Our similarities on the inside are often more important than our similarities on the outside. We know and associate with people who complement our personality and share our lifestyle and interests. We relate to people who think the way we do.

Psychographics groups people based on internal characteristics we can't see. Such characteristics include personality, lifestyle, social class, and interests. The purpose of grouping people according to these characteristics is to identify common internal needs you can serve.

People with a psychographic of achievement will have different wants compared to those who are just surviving[63]. They may want things—perhaps luxury automobiles—that reflect their

---

62 (Income, n.d.)

63 (Kotler & Armstrong, 2008)

accomplishments. In fact, they may use the attainment of things to establish their status.

Serving people based on their psychographics is difficult. People don't typically wear their psychographics on their sleeve. That is, people don't usually reveal their social class, lifestyle, or personality characteristics. You have to determine these things by observing what they say and do.

Get your customers to talk about themselves, and that will help you to identify their psychographics. To begin with, you might ask your customers about their goals to gather clues about their lifestyle.

As an example, if you are a financial advisor and your customer tells you they are just trying to get by, that obviously means they're in survival mode. But if they tell you they need to figure out how to retire in the Bahamas, then they are obviously an achiever. So you'd want to tailor your investment advice accordingly.

Notice the customer's response to questions. If they are gregarious, then that has implications for how you serve them. Friendly people are sociable, and they will respond to that orientation. But whatever the customer's personality characteristics are, try to group customers with others who are similar and then determine how they want to be served.

Behavior

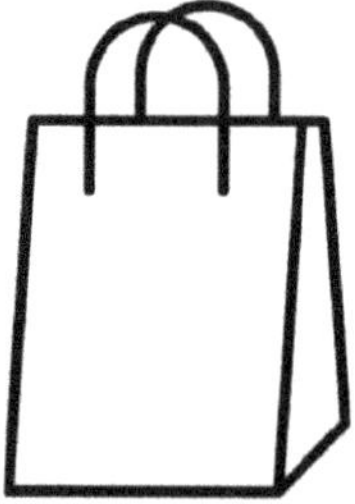

We have a saying in marketing that "the greatest predictor of future behavior is past performance." If you want to guess how people will behave, just look at what they've done in the past, and you will have a pretty good idea of what they will do in the future.

Why?

Most people don't change that much, which makes them surprisingly predictable. You can use that insight to serve them.

Marketing scientists use advanced mathematics to predict what people will do in the future based on what they have done in the past. They look at what people bought, what circumstances drove customers to buy, and their usage rates (e.g., heavy user versus light user). Once they know these things, they use this information to determine what the customer will buy in the future.

Generally speaking, you should serve people by providing them with the things or experiences they like and use repeatedly. That's pretty simple. You just need to know what to look for.

Study your customer's behavior. What do they do? Do they have certain hobbies? How do they respond to certain situations? Do they like certain products? Are they obsessive about something? We need to know.

Cater to your customer's preferences. If, for instance, you know that your customer enjoys fine dining, you may want to take him to an upscale restaurant or, better yet, you could create such a restaurant and invite him to visit it.

As another example, consider the shopping behavior of people. Research suggests that women place far more emphasis on the relationship aspect of shopping compared to men[64]. For women, the sales associate makes or breaks the shopping experience. Why? Women assign great importance to interpersonal relationships.

---

[64] ('Men Buy, Women Shop': The Sexes Have Different Priorities When Walking Down the Aisles, 2007)

In contrast, men don't shop. Men enter a store with a singular mission in mind. They know what they want. They value someone who can help them find the item so they can get out of the store as quickly as possible.

Men want to run in and run out. If the grocery store had a drive-through, men would use it.

Use behavior to serve your customers the way they want to be served.

Geography

Geography can be an important way to group and serve people. For example, you wouldn't want to try to sell snow shovels to people in Florida. Floridians don't get much snow. Conversely, don't expect people in the northern parts of China to buy lots of flip-flops in the middle of winter. It's freezing then.

The geographical differences among people aren't confined solely to those with a vastly different longitude and latitude. We can often find big differences between zip codes in the same city. For instance, one zip code might have people with an average annual household income, while another might have people who are among the richest five percent.

Beyond climate and income differences, you'll find sociopolitical differences in geographic areas. Sociopolitical segments combine both social and political factors[65]. For instance,

[65] (sociopolitical, n.d.)

the deep South of the United States is socially conservative, while the Pacific Northwest is liberal. The politics follows, suggesting that the South is predominantly Republican, while the Northwest is heavily populated with Democrats. Such regional differences will have implications for consumer tastes and predilections.

Use geography to help identify customer segments that you can serve.

Life Events

We all have important life events that usher in a new stream of needs. Having a baby is a good example. When the baby is born, you need baby furniture, clothing, food, toys, and childcare services, among other things. You could build an entire business catering to the needs of people based on a single life event.

Life events are major milestones in a person's life that often change a person's perspective and needs completely. If your customer has had a significant life event you can identify, then this information will help you relate to them and perhaps serve them.

Some examples of life events are:

- Graduation from high school or college
- First job
- Marriage
- Purchase of first home
- Birth of children
- Retirement

If you've gone through any of these life events, you can use that experience to understand your customers. If not, take some time to familiarize yourself with major life events. It will help you spot a need you can serve.

The great thing about serving people based on life events is that needs are fairly obvious. Moreover, many times customers go through some advance planning before the big event. You can use that information to serve people on a one-on-one basis.

Serving large segments of people based on a life event is difficult though because you don't always know when people are going to have the life event. That information is reserved for close friends and family. The use of social media, however, is changing what's possible.

Customers like to post all kinds of stuff about their life on sites such as Facebook.

Generally speaking, the best way to serve segments of people based on life events is to organize your service to them—perhaps via the Internet—and then advertise it. When the customer has a need, they will think of you.

Value

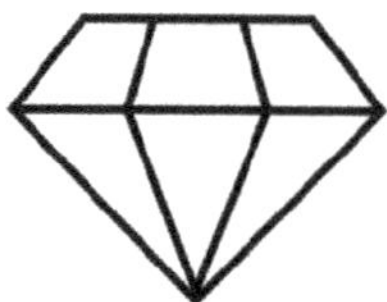

An old marketing adage states "eighty percent of the revenue a company generates comes from twenty percent of the customers." My experience confirms this point. Even though this is a widely known precept, many smart business people still do not focus enough on finding ways to better serve the top twenty percent. Crazy, isn't it?

Everyone should be focused on his top customers, but you have to identify them first. The best way to do that is to group your customers according to their value to you.

Not all customers are worth the same thing. Some customers are worth more than others. That is, some customers provide you more value. You'd make a big mistake to overlook that simple point.

Why?

If you lose them, you lose their value to you.

You can segment your customers by the value they generate for you. That value can be a number of things. It can be the physical or monetary value they generate for you such as revenue or profit. It can be intangible things such as emotional or social benefits to you. Whatever you value most, segment your customers according to that value and then make sure the customers who provide you the most value get preferred service.

So, what do you value the most?

An acquaintance once told me that no success can compensate for failure in the home. When I heard him say that, I thought he'd probably change his perspective if I added a few more zeros after his annual income. But I realized that this was a very wise man who was making a statement that clearly defined his priorities. His family was the most important thing in his life, so when the going got tough, he would choose his family as the top priority. We all need to get to a point where we know our values so we can determine our priority segments.

Your priorities in life are determined by your organizational or personal values. You can think of your values as an unconscious set of criteria that you use to make decisions. Your values are what you really want out of life or business. An example of some values is listed in the table below.

Example List of Personal Values[66]

Accomplishment, Success
Accountability
Accuracy
Adventure
All for one & one for all
Beauty
Calm, quietude, peace
Challenge
Change
Cleanliness, orderliness
Collaboration
Commitment
Communication
Community
Competence
Competition
Concern for others
Connection
Content over form
Continuous improvement
Cooperation
Coordination
Creativity
Customer satisfaction
Decisiveness
Delight of being, joy
Democracy
Discipline
Discovery
Diversity
Ease of Use
Efficiency
Equality
Excellence
Fairness
Faith
Faithfulness
Family
Flair
Family feeling
Freedom
Friendship
Fun
Global view
Good will
Goodness
Gratitude
Hard work
Harmony
Honesty
Honor
Improvement
Independence
Individuality
Inner peace, calm, quietude
Innovation
Integrity
Intensity
Justice
Knowledge
Leadership
Love, Romance
Loyalty
Maximum utilization (of time, resources)
Meaning
Merit
Money
Openness
Patriotism
Peace, Non-violence
Perfection
Personal Growth
Pleasure
Power
Practicality
Preservation
Privacy
Progress
Prosperity, Wealth
Punctuality
Quality of work
Regularity
Reliability
Resourcefulness
Respect for others
Responsiveness
Results-oriented
Rule of Law
Safety
Satisfying others
Security
Self-givingness
Self-reliance
Self-thinking
Service (to others, society)
Simplicity
Skill
Solving Problems
Speed
Spirit in life (using)
Stability
Standardization
Status
Strength
Succeed; A will to-
Success, Achievement
Systemization
Teamwork
Timeliness
Tolerance
Tradition
Tranquility
Trust
Truth
Unity
Variety
Wisdom

66 (gurusoftware.com, n.d.)

Most of us don't spend much time thinking about our values. Instead, our values develop throughout our life based on our experiences with people, communities, and institutions. In effect, your value system develops in response to life. The operative word is *response*.

For the most part, your personal values aren't something you have consciously chosen. You probably didn't wake up this morning and decide that you would now have compassion for others or that you value innovation. Rather, you learned to value such things only because you learned the benefits that such ideas can generate.

Your value system guides your decisions. If you don't take charge of your value system, it will control you.

Think about money. If you value money more than customers, you might take advantage of them to get their money. In the short run you might make some money, but over time you will lose out. You will lose the customers who paid you.

If we want control over our life, the first order of business is to understand how our life is being controlled. To do that, you need to understand your value system.

Use the list of values printed here and choose your top ten. After you've done that, rank them from one to ten. What values came first? Are those congruent with your customer's needs? If they are not in accord, you may be working against your own best interests without even knowing it.

In my line of business, I know people in sales who are willing to throw their mama under a bus just to close a deal. For those salespeople, it's all about the deal. Funny thing is, those same people also have the darndest time trying to repeat their occasional super success and retain their customers. Instead they are off chasing the next opportunity. They forget to take care of their current customers.

Arrange your value system so it supports both you and your customers.

Connecting the Dots

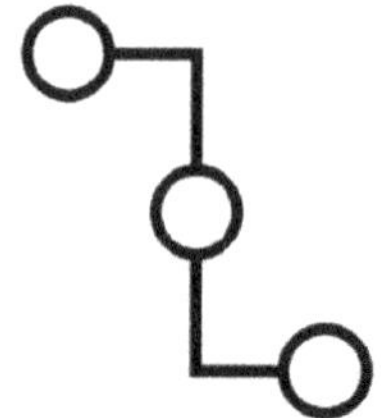

We have covered a lot of different ways to segment customers. Each of them will help you fine-tune your service. And they can be used in combination. You can connect the dots among the segmentation types to further determine whom you serve. For example, you can include in one customer segment all the paying customers who make at least $100,000 a year—the ones most valuable to you—who are achievers, who like to buy fine wine, and who live in the Southwest. In one stroke, I linked all of the segment types together.

The more detailed you make the segment, the narrower your focus will be on those you serve. That isn't a bad thing. I know a guy who made a killing selling pet supplies to people who owned a pet pig. Well, maybe not a killing, but he seems to squeal out a nice living.

The point is that you can make a comfortable living when you clarify the type of people you want to serve.

CHAPTER 8

Opinions Matter

My wife shops at least once a day. That's once more than I shop in a day, so, right or wrong, that seems like a lot, but what do I know.

I marvel at my wife's shopping fortitude. She is like a skilled hunter, lurking behind the store's shelving with debit card aimed at any deal. She often comes home with all kinds of trinkets and gizmos in bags thrown over her shoulder, as if she had just killed some wild animal on the plains of Africa. She is the *bargain hunter.*

I am privileged to be my wife's audience while she models various items she purchased. I often feel as if I'm in the audience of the Home Shopping Network or QVC as she spouts off all the features and functions of each item. Sometimes, I think that she has actually memorized the marketing mumbo jumbo she read on the package or label. It's a real hoot to watch her perform.

Curiously enough, with all the shopping comes great wisdom. For instance, my wife will sometimes buy two of the same thing, especially shoes. For years, I could never figure out why until I finally asked her.

"Ah, honey? Why did you buy two of the same pair of shoes?"

She told me that she doesn't want to risk the chance of the shoes being discontinued, so she buys two pairs, just in case. It's like an insurance program for shoppers I guess, and she reasons that if she ever wants to, she can just return the second pair and get her money back. The only downside is that my basement feels like an unofficial distribution center for some big retailer.

I'm convinced that my wife is the unsuspecting victim of the old slogan "Hurry now while supplies last." And for that reason, I'm certain that most marketers would love her as much as I do—that is until they learn that she returns almost as much as she buys. In fact, she returns things to the store almost every day, which makes her one demanding shopper.

I often tag along with my wife when she goes to the store, feeling like one of those native bearers in Africa who carry all the gear on their head as they follow their European tourists on a safari. As I do my duty, I lug her latest kill on my back until she commands me to drop it on a customer service counter. Then I retreat to a safe distance and watch the transaction unfold before me.

Almost every time I repeat this routine with my wife, the customer-service person will invariably ask her the reason for the return. I am often amazed at the level of detail my wife provides. She will say something like, "The zipper on these pants catches when I pull it up at the wrong angle." The customer-service person commiserates with her, recognizing that such an experience is less than acceptable. Sadly, for the manufacturer, that information seems to get "lost in transaction," rarely making its way back to them. The manufacturer will lose my wife as a customer without ever knowing it.

You know, that's how a lot of things go in life. If you've ever interviewed for a job and failed to make the cut, you rarely learn the reason why. If you lose a sale to someone else, you are similarly unlikely to get the "real deal." Sometimes people even lose their significant other to someone else without ever knowing why until it's too late.

What about you? Do your customers want a refund? Are they tired of your defective ways? Have they told you that they "don't buy it"? Do they seem dissatisfied with you? Have they called you a "reject"?

If you don't know the answers, then you run the risk of being *returned*, or, worse, you may be accused of being defective and perhaps even hazardous to use!

Unlike a defective zipper on the pair of pants my wife returned, you can change your defective ways. You just need to know what they are. So, I have a question for you. Have you ever asked one of your customers how you are doing?

If you're married, consider your spouse, for instance. When was the last time you asked him or her how you are doing as a mate? How would you score on a scale of one to ten, with one being really bad and ten being really great? Do you know?

If in your most intimate relationships you don't know how you're doing, don't be surprised when your significant other suddenly leaves you.

The same holds true for your paying customers. Don't expect them to hang around if they aren't thoroughly satisfied with your service. You need to ask them how you're doing. You need to know if they want a refund.

We somehow think we can be successful without the least bit of concern about what our customers think. Even more interesting, when we do get feedback, we often feel defensive and angry. We don't want to hear that something is wrong with us. Instead we are content with our defective ways, so we go on telling ourselves "nothing is wrong with me. If they don't like it, they can leave. They have the problem, not me."

I have a message for you: you're not perfect. You have all kinds of flaws, and some of them rub people the wrong way. If you are going to improve, you have to identify those flaws. You need your customer's feedback to find them.

To be at your best, you must be ready and willing to get customer feedback so you can improve yourself as a "product." The more often you do this, the faster you will learn what to change and improve to become a better product for your customers.

Regardless of whether you are a big-time CEO or a small business owner, lawyer, or a professional clown, you have to be open to and actively seeking customer feedback. The more successful you become, the more direct feedback you will need. This is because everyone subordinate to you will often mask what is really going on in the marketplace or how the marketplace truly feels about your service. Don't think you are above asking for feedback.

A.G. Lafely, the former CEO of Procter & Gamble, was renowned for focusing on customers and asking them for their opinions and suggestions. He would walk the barrios of Brazil looking for ways to better serve his customers. His mantra was the "customer is the boss." His philosophy helped Procter & Gamble consistently outperform competitors in terms of profits and stock price for many, many years.

We need to embrace customer feedback. We need to seek it out. So, roll up your sleeves and tell the world to "let me have it."

Your Feelings After Receiving Negative Feedback

SMACK! BOOM! POW! At least that's what it's going to feel like when you get feedback from some of your customers because "you asked for it." But that's good. It will probably knock some sense into you.

Your tendency may be to fight back, but after all, you're only human. When attacked, verbally or otherwise, it is only natural to become defensive or try to retaliate. But you can't do that because you need people to be honest with you in the future. If you become defensive with customers, you'll only drive them away.

Research has shown that businesspeople who ask their customers for feedback actually improve their ratings[67]. This means that customer satisfaction improves when you ask for feedback. So why not try it? If nothing else, you'll improve customer satisfaction. Even better, you might find a way to improve your service, or discover a new one, all while claiming The Hidden Fortune of Service.

---

67 (Simonson & Ofir, 2005)

Getting the Customer to Talk

People like to express their opinions because they feel flattered by your interest in their point of view. Why? People want to be esteemed, and when you ask them for their opinion, you make them feel that way. When you are ready to ask customers for feedback, they will be happy to give it because you are serving their needs.

The simplest way to get feedback from customers is to ask them for it. A number of methods exist to gather feedback, however. For instance, you can interview your customers one-on-one; you can conduct focus groups; you can use projective techniques; you can use ethnography; and you can survey them. Each technique has value at the appropriate place and time. I will discuss using the interview and the survey because these should be your foundation for gathering information. And a life of collecting feedback will produce a wealth of ideas you can use to capture The Hidden Fortune of Service.

The President and CEO of Walmart U.S. posted a message on LinkedIn. One of the company's customer service associates, Christina, identified a need for an affordable diaper option for families on the go. In response, Walmart developed a $0.98 5-pack of diapers. Pretty cool!

So, how did Christina do it? She listened to the needs of different families and then she convinced the company to develop something that would serve those needs.

It's too early to tell how well Christina's product idea will sell. However, she is now memorialized in this book for her act of service. She has benefited from The Hidden Fortune of Service.

You might ask me, "If customer feedback is so important, why didn't Steve Jobs, the former CEO of Apple, Inc., spend more time asking for it? I mean, Jobs was wildly successful, but he didn't bother to ask consumers what they wanted."

Jobs once responded to questions about Apple's customer-feedback efforts with his own question: "Did Alexander Graham Bell do any market research before he invented the telephone?" His point is that when you are inventing something that hasn't existed before, you can't ask people if they want it. Touché, Mr. Jobs.

While people like Steve Jobs have prescience and insight about what people will use, the reality is that most of us don't. Why do I say that? Because sixty-five percent of all products and services fail[68]. The main reason they fail: consumers didn't buy it.

Why didn't they buy?

Because the customer didn't need it, of course. Then why did the inventor create something that customers didn't need? The answer is the inventor didn't bother to get enough customer feedback.

Don't be a statistic. Ask the customer for input.

Interviews

[68] (Adams, n.d.)

Interviews with customers are perhaps the most effective method of gathering information about their needs.

In fact, in just ten interviews, with ten different customers, you can identify about ninety percent of the market's needs for a service[69]. That is, you can identify ninety percent of the needs of all people by interviewing only ten people in the target segment. This is a way to gather a tremendous amount of insight for relatively little work, which makes the interview one of the best methods for collecting feedback.

Conducting interviews isn't very complicated, but you need to give it some thought and plan out what you want to get feedback about. You don't need to make it formal and you don't need to tell anyone that you are interviewing them.

Give customers only a brief explanation, saying that you'd like their opinion about your service or a new product idea you have. This will help the customer understand what you are trying to do, and it will also help them think of ways to help you. Customers are the best source of ideas, and they will let you know how to help you help them, so let them in on your game plan.

Next, you want to ask customers some carefully worded questions that will elicit their needs, wants, and suggestions. Frame your questions in a positive way. For instance, ask customers to give you some ideas about how you can improve the value of your product or how you can help them as the customer. This will help you identify ideas that will provide new value.

If you want to identify breakthrough new service ideas, then you need to interview customers as a natural part of every conversation. Get in the habit of interviewing every customer during every conversation. Identify what they need, want, and

---

[69] (Ulrich & Eppinger, 2004)

desire. With each interaction, you increase the odds of discovering a breakthrough new service or one that you can sell.

The founder of NIKE, Phil Knight, got the idea for his company while selling shoes out of the trunk of his car. Knight's idea for NIKE was grounded in feedback he received from a University of Oregon running coach who was looking for a lighter and more durable running shoe[70]. Knight set out to serve this need by creating a better running shoe, and in the process, he built an apparel empire that today generates $21 billion in sales annually[71].

Surveys

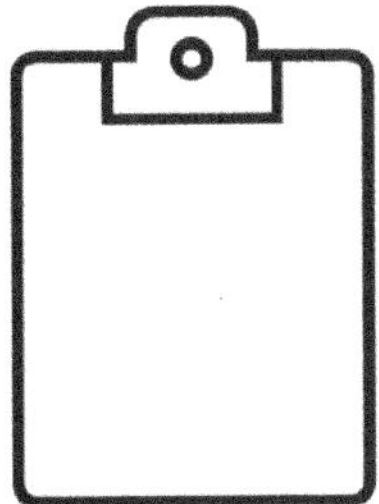

You survey customers for three important reasons. The first is to determine what percentage of the population shares something in common. This is important when you need to know how many people would be interested in something you have to sell. If sixty percent or more are interested, you probably have a very good idea for a new product or service.

The second reason you survey customers is to solicit their opinion or feedback on something. By using surveys, you can

[70] (Nike's Heritage, n.d.)

[71] (Yahoo! Finance, n.d.)

collect feedback on new ideas or services you have developed. The responses will help you determine if you have a winner or not.

Third, some people don't like to give others negative feedback, but since surveys can be taken without disclosing identity, they are an especially useful tool.

Anyone can create a survey. But to be useful, your survey needs to do two important things.

First, your survey needs to capture feedback from the right group of people. You don't want to survey just anybody. You want to survey people you serve today or those you would like to serve in the future.

The second important aspect of designing your survey is making sure it elicits honest and useful feedback from customers. To do that, you need to construct good questions that are written in simple, unambiguous, and objective language.

Questions may ask people to indicate yes or no or true or false. The survey may also ask the subject to choose from a multiple-choice list, rate things on a scale of one to ten, or write a brief response. The objective of such questioning techniques is to simplify the survey for the respondent and maximize the probability that you will get accurate and useful data.

Once the survey is ready, you will have to distribute it. You can use online survey tools to reach your customers. Online surveys allow customers to complete a survey without using too much effort and time. For that reason, this is the best way to conduct a survey.

You should gather feedback from customers regularly if you want to identify new ways to serve them. This is how you'll find ideas that serve the largest number of customers.

Wallowing in Your Feedback

The feedback you generate from your research is invaluable, but some of it may also be painful to hear. Nobody wants to know how bad they are, and you won't like hearing it either. But you can't hope to change yourself as a product unless you can take the bad with the good.

Accept your feedback for what it is—an opportunity to see yourself through the lens of your customers. Do that, and then get busy organizing the feedback so you can start to use it.

Try to group your feedback into categories so you can discover any recurring themes. For instance, if several people tell you that you are inconsiderate, hurtful, mean, or indifferent, you could place that feedback in a category named "Insensitive."

Take the time to pore over your feedback and reflect on it. Then correct whatever caused your customers to say unpleasant things about you. On the plus side, when you get good feedback from a lot of customers, you'll know that you're doing a good job. Whatever you did to get that positive feedback, keep doing it.

Be excited to get customer feedback. Just like Phil Knight of NIKE, you might find a billion-dollar idea for a new product or service if you pay attention to what people told you.

Chapter 9

Inside the Circle

"I want a refund," my wife said to me.

"What?" I asked.

I was laying on the couch. I had my feet on the ottoman, my right arm behind my head, and my left arm extended toward the television with the remote in hand.

She said, "I paid too much for you. You cost me more than you're worth."

I turned to her, perplexed, as I came out of a TV-induced coma. I quickly pieced together what she was getting at. My wife was talking to me in a way that I could understand because I'm a marketer by trade, so I tend to look at things in terms of customer versus product.

My wife was telling me, in effect, that my cost outweighed my benefits as a husband, that she wasn't getting good value for her money.

At first, I thought, "My wife must be the smartest person I've ever met. She's able to talk to me in a language I can understand."

I started to think that this was a fun way to interact, so I went along with the game of "I am the product" and "she is the customer."

I sat up and clicked off the TV.

"Okay, I get it. On a scale of one to ten, how am I doing as a husband?"

"Honestly?"

"Of course. Let me have it."

"I'd give you a five or six."

I was stunned. I had thought things were good, but now I hear that I'm below average. Apparently, I was doing just enough to keep her around. What would happen if she found a better product? I would lose everything!

I have to improve my score, or I would lose my wife, my most important customer. Then, something worse happened. My son told me he wanted to take me back to Walmart to return me and get a new Daddy because I wouldn't change the channel to let him watch his favorite TV show.

At this point, I hit rock bottom. I thought, "I'm a return." I knew I had to do something quick or I'd end up back in the "meat market."

I began my journey to change my product by asking my wife questions about what her needs were and what she wanted in life. I used my knowledge of market research to get at the root of what she really wanted in life and from me.

I discovered all kinds of hidden needs, wants, and desires. I realized that my features and benefits as a husband/product were out of whack. I wasn't delivering on the assumed value proposition, which is to say that she *wasn't getting what she had bargained for* when she married me. I started to see through her eyes that I was even *defective* and at times *hazardous to use*!

My wife's feedback was hard to take. I thought I was a wonderful husband, but my view was at odds with reality. I had to change, and I did. I improved myself as a product and my score as a husband. My wife now gives me eights and nines.

You can improve your product no matter who you are or what your circumstances are when you focus on the needs of others.

Many people have transformed themselves in the midst of challenging circumstances. You will find many examples the world over.

Farrah Gray was an inner-city child who grew up in the housing projects in Chicago during the 1980s. Life was tough for Gray. He would say of his life back then that there were many days when "the only thing in the refrigerator was the light that came on[72]."

But at age six, he got an idea of painting rocks and selling them as doorstops and bookends to make money to buy food. At age thirteen, he started Farr-out Foods, targeting young people. At fourteen, his company generated $1.5 million in sales, making him a millionaire[73].

You can change your circumstances by becoming a better product to serve people.

Before you can improve your product, you have to know what to change. Before you can know what to change, you have to analyze your product results. To do that, you must do something that is very hard: you need to be honest with yourself. Each of us needs to take a long, hard look at the results we have produced, and the feedback we've received, to identify the reasons for why we aren't where we want to be.

Pick an area of your life and evaluate your results as a product. I'll help. Let's pick money. If you have enough, great. If you don't, then I want you to say, "I don't have the amount of money I need and want." Be honest with yourself. That will make it easier to change.

---

[72] (Fastenberg, 2011)

[73] (Farrah Gray, n.d.)

I want you to think about the root cause of your situation. In fact, write down ten reasons why you don't have enough money. When you're done, come back to the book, and we'll evaluate the results.

Tick, tock, tick, tock, tick, tock . . .

I hope you took the time to write down all the reasons that prevent you from getting all the money you need and want. That means you're serious and want to improve your money situation.

Now that you have your ten reasons written down, I want you to do something extra. Divide your answers into groups so you can analyze your results. If any of your reasons concern other people, put them into a separate group and name it "Customer group." If any of the reasons relate to you, put those into another group or box and name it "Product group."

I want you to look at the reasons in the Product group. Focus on them. Notice the words you used to describe these reasons and the emotions you have about them. Put down this book and consider these words carefully. When you're done, go back and draw a big X over those answers. Why? None of those reasons matters. You as the product are not the reason you don't have enough money. Unless you work at the U.S. mint, *you* don't make money. You need *customers* to give you money, and therefore *they* are the reason that you don't have enough.

I use the term *customer* liberally to apply to employers, coworkers, and of course real paying customers. Using the word *customer* in this way certainly stretches the definition of a customer, but that doesn't matter. The point of using this term is that it assigns importance to people around you and correctly places you as a servant to them. We need to adopt this philosophy and change the way we look at the world if we want to become more successful. When you change your perspective and begin to serve the people you circled as customers, you'll change your financial situation. But if you make money your focus, you will never have enough, and you might be tempted to do something unethical, immoral, or illegal.

Consider some of the scandals of many high-profile financiers, hedge fund managers, and corporations. They all cheated people to get money, and they got in trouble for it.

Let's jump back to your list of reasons in the customer group. Circle those who have a direct influence on giving money to you or your company. Ask yourself what you could do for them that would help them or improve their life.

Think about the customers who actually buy or use your products and services. If you don't serve them better than the competition, you will lose their money, and you will have even less than you have now. I'm amazed about how many people don't understand this principle, so let me make it simple. If the customer doesn't buy, you don't eat. Period. Help your customers improve their life in some meaningful way, and they will reward you for it.

You could try to cheat your way to success by providing something to a customer that doesn't deliver value. You can make a buck for a while this way, but eventually customers will catch on, and the word will get out that you don't provide any value.

Just one dissatisfied customer can do great harm to your reputation. They can share their poor opinion of you with hundreds or thousands of others in no time at all. This will impact your opportunities almost immediately.

If one dissatisfied customer can have this much of an influence, imagine what would happen if you had several dissatisfied customers. You could destroy your chances of success. You have to provide value as a product to all of your customers.

If you work for someone else, then you probably wrote down another important customer—your employer or your boss. Yes, your employer is a customer. You do work for him, and he pays you for it. He buys your services.

Your boss is one of your most important customers. He has the power to give you a merit increase, a raise, a bonus, or a promotion. You want to make sure you give your boss a hundred percent.

If your boss is going to give you more money, you have to help him achieve his goals so he can get his bonus and make more money. Your boss depends on you, and you depend on him. If he fails, you fail.

Never forget that your boss is your customer and you are the product. You want him to buy more of your time and give you more money for what you give him.

Your boss doesn't owe you anything except to treat you with respect and pay you a fair wage. In exchange, you are responsible to give him a hundred percent. Do anything less, and your customer, the boss, will pass you over for raises and promotion.

So far, we have discussed two possible customer types. Did you write down any other customer types? If so, spend some time thinking about them and what you can do for them to provide value. You will find an idea for how you can make more money.

But what about the people who are not included in your group of customers? Did you list only those customers you serve today? Did you list all of your noncustomers or your prospects? If you didn't, why not? Did you think that you can make more money only by serving the same customers as you always have?

You and I both know that to make a lot of money, you have to serve a lot of customers. Change your thinking. You can find other customers to serve and thereby expand the universe of customers who pay you. That will increase your chances of making more money.

In short, you must identify the customers you want. Study their needs and find a way to serve them better than the next person, and you will make more money.

Now that we've discussed the importance of the customer, let's go back to all the reasons you crossed out. All of them were about you. I don't want to dismiss these reasons completely because sometimes you need to improve your product to get more customers and make more money. That might mean you need to upgrade your skills. If that is the case, make the investment and improve your product. But do it for your customers. Listen to what they want from you and then give it to them.

Yet most of the time you will find that if you spend too much time thinking about yourself and why you aren't good enough, you will forget your customers. Your customers in turn, will find someone else who will serve them just as well, even though you might be the best one for the job. Make sure the customer knows you're "open for business." Don't close any doors.

We have talked about customers as a source of money, but not all of your customers will give you money. Sometimes you will need to give them money. If you're an employer, some of your most important customers are your employees.

Your employees can help you innovate new products, make you more efficient, and help you achieve sales growth.

Without them, you don't have a chance. You need to think about your employees as customers to get the best out of them. Why? If you don't make your employees happy, then they will never give you their very best. You will then forfeit all they have to offer. If you don't believe this, then you need to study the Toyota Corporation.

Toyota is now one of the world's largest automakers in terms of net worth, revenue, and profits. Toyota has been a leader in the auto industry since the 1960s and has consistently produced top-quality products. Toyota has won awards from J.D. Power and Associates' annual initial quality rankings in three car segments for 2008, four car segments in 2007, eleven segments during 2006, and fifteen of the top model segments in 2005[74,75,76].

For years the heart of Toyota's success in manufacturing quality products is its philosophy. Team members serve the next person on the production line as their customer, so they will not pass a defective part on to that customer. If a team member finds a problem with a part of the automobile, then the team member stops the line and corrects the problem before the vehicle goes farther down the line[77].

Think about that for a minute. The most successful auto company in the world has institutionalized a process where everyone in the assembly line is a customer, including the person who buys the product at the end of it. Unless you think of your employees and everyone in your supply chain as a customer, you will never learn to match the success that Toyota has achieved.

Although Toyota has lost its luster recently, we can't dispute the many years of its focus on customers. Let's hope they solve their problems and get back on the road to building great cars.

---

74 (Karoub, nl.d.)

75 (reuters.com, n.d.)

76 (J.D. Power and Associates Reports: HUMMER, Nissan and Scion Show Strong Improvement, n.d.)

77 (htt7)

Chapter 10

Re-engineer Your Mind

You are a product of your environment, your genetics, your experiences, your education, and your thoughts. Whether it is your income, your health, your relationships, or any other part of your life, the results you produce are completely expected and predictable because they are based on you as the product.

You could say you are perfectly designed to get the results you have been getting in life. The question you must ask yourself is whether or not you like those results. Do you like the results you have been getting in life? Are you satisfied with your career? If you're not, you have to change your product. That is, you have to change yourself.

Think about this in business terms. You can't have customers unless you have a good product. When you serve everyone like a customer, you are providing them with a product by the things you do for them that they need, want, and perhaps can't get anywhere else.

As a product, your primary role is to figure out what your customers need. The ability to spot needs is the single greatest skill you will ever learn. Doing this takes practice. If you make the effort to develop this skill and you become good at identifying the needs of your customers, you will find an opportunity to gain The Hidden Fortune of Service.

The first step in learning to recognize and serve customer needs is to learn how to identify with the customer. When we learn how to do that, we are able to understand the world from their perspective.

If you've ever received good customer service, then you probably know how good that feels. The best customer service comes from those who anticipate your needs and go out of their way to satisfy them. You need to pay attention though, and be especially aware of how to anticipate a person's needs. You have to get into their shoes and imagine what it means to be that person. You have to identify with them. You have to empathize with them.

The ability to empathize with another person is related to a concept called the "Theory of Mind" (ToM). The Theory of Mind is the ability of a person to infer what another person is thinking and feeling. That's what helps us to get into someone else's shoes.

We all use this ability to understand the mental state of others and what might cause their behavior. We can use the Theory of Mind to explain and predict people's behavior.

Being able to understand people's thinking and feelings means that you must be able to recognize that other people have a different perspective or mental representation of the world. It also means you must be able to maintain different representations of the world simultaneously[78].

And as research shows, such a mental ability often leads to being able to truly feel the pain of others.

In a research study done at the University College of London, British researchers recruited sixteen couples (male and female) to

---

78 (Theory of Mind, n.d.)

test empathy. For the research study, each couple was hooked up to a device that would give them an electrical shock at the discretion of the researcher.

The female was placed next to a magnetic resonance imaging (MRI) scanner to monitor her brain activity, but she could still see the hand of her male partner. Both male and female were able to see a computer screen, which served to inform both of them about which one would get the next shock and roughly how painful it would be.

When the female was shocked, the MRI showed her entire pain network activated, as expected. Curiously, when the women knew that their male partner would be shocked and how badly it would hurt, the MRI showed that similar parts of her pain network activated[79].

In a separate study by University College of London, researchers set up an experiment to test the empathy of both men and women toward strangers. The experiment involved thirty-two volunteers who first witnessed people play a financial game in which some players were fair, and others were unfair.

Later, the volunteers were placed in an MRI scanner, where they watched as both the fair and unfair players received a mild electrical shock. When a fair player was shocked, the MRI recorded an effect in the observer's brain[80]. This clearly demonstrates that when we empathize, we can feel the pain of others.

Let's take a science lesson for a moment to understand what's going on in our brain when we feel empathy and see what it means. First, we should note that many parts of the brain are involved in empathy, but let's start with the limbic system.

The limbic system is considered to be the emotional part of our brain. The front part of the insular cortex and the cingulate cortex

[79] (Do couples truly share pain? Studies probe brain, empathy, 2004)

[80] (htt8)

are two parts of the limbic system that activate the feeling of empathy. The front part of the insular cortex is underneath the cingulate cortex and it is activated when we feel emotional pain ourselves or empathize with another person. The cingulate cortex rests on top of the insular cortex, and it too appears to be involved in our caring for other people. You should think of both of these areas as the place where the raw emotion of empathy is generated. It's where mirror neurons live. Mirror neurons help you understand the feelings of others.

Key Parts os the Brain Related to Empathy[81]

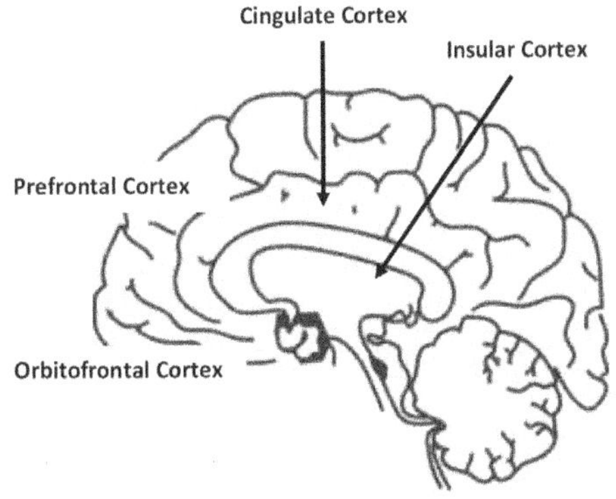

Another area of the brain named the prefrontal cortex is used for the higher functions of thought. It activates when we concentrate on our own mental state and that of others[82]. This area of the brain is located behind the forehead at about the level of your eyebrows.

The prefrontal cortex is very important because it appears to be a critical part of the brain that's associated with empathy. It's our filter for the world and where most of our complex thinking takes place.

---

[81] (htt9)

[82] (Hanson, 2007)

A research study on empathy was conducted to determine if the same areas of the brain are activated in teenagers and adults. The research showed that while adults clearly used the parts of the brain just described, teenagers used a different part of the brain named the superior temporal sulcus, which is part of the brain used to predict future actions based on past actions[83]. This suggests that teenagers can understand the consequences of their actions and how it might affect those around them, but they may not understand or care how those people feel about it.

Other studies of teenagers have shown that they are prone to taking unnecessary risks, largely because their prefrontal cortex is not yet developed and therefore cannot reason as well as an adult's regarding consequences of behavior[84]. In fact, the teenage mind does not appear to be as well connected because the synapses or "connections" are not yet well defined.

So, what does all of this mean? Your brain must be fully developed in order to have true empathy for others.

We can develop our brain in two ways. The first is a function of time, that is, we can wait until our mind is fully developed. The second is to make a conscious effort.

The first step in developing your level of empathy is to become self-aware, to understand your own senses and emotional responses. You can develop your brain and level of empathy by simply focusing in this way.

Take the insular cortex, for instance. The insular cortex is involved in interoception, or sensing the internal state of your body. This part of the brain registers the feeling of getting a "gut reaction" to something. By learning to stop and reflect on your natural visceral responses, you can develop your insular cortex and thus learn to become more empathetic.

---

[83] (findcounseling.com, n.d.)

[84] (Edmonds, n.d.)

You can also develop the cingulate cortex by learning to concentrate on one thing at a time for a long period of time. By doing so, you will strengthen your cingulate cortex and your ability to empathize.

The prefrontal cortex is best developed through introspection focused on observing, investigating, and reflecting on your own internal state.

Areas of the Brain and Development of Empathy

	Purpose	Activation	Development
Cingulate Cortex	Involved with emotion formation and processing, learning, and memory, and is also important for executive function.	When we have to deal with emotional consequences of actions, learning from those consequences.	Concentrate on one thing at a time for a long period of time (meditate).
Insular Cortex	Involved in interoception or sensing the internal state of your body.	When we feel emotional pain ourselves or empathize with another person.	Stop and reflect on your natural visceral responses to life.
Prefrontal Cortex	Used for higher functions and thought.	When we concentrate on own natural states or that of others; when we have to solve problems.	Focus on introspection by observing, investigating, and reflecting on your own internal state.
Orbitofrontal Cortex	Enables individuals to adapt their behavior in response to unexpected rewards or challenges.	When individuals must choose a course of action to receive a reward rather than punishment by other people.	Imagine the response from people based on how you treat them, and then behave positively toward people to get a reward ("play the game").

Playing the Game

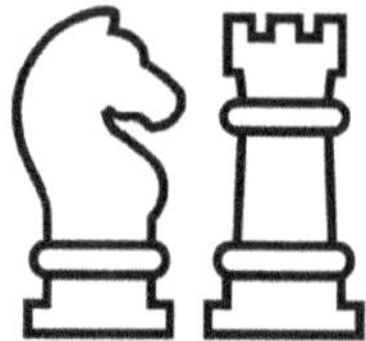

Has anyone ever told you that in order to get ahead in life you need to "play the game?" If not, let me explain the concept to you.

Playing the game means you follow the rules and conventions of people, or organizations, to get ahead. The reward could be a promotion, it could be more money, or it could even be a date with a great looking person.

Playing the game could be very important to your future success. Why? It causes you to focus on behaviors that will yield a reward and shun those behaviors that bring pain.

The orbitofrontal cortex is the part of the brain that helps you determine social rewards and punishments. This area of the brain helps you figure out what to do to get ahead, and it also helps you figure out how your behavior is impacting customers. If you want to develop this part of the brain, play the game. Give your customers what they need and want. Over time, you will cause a psychological and physiological change that will help you improve your ability to serve and succeed.

The best way to develop all of the areas of your brain that are responsible for empathy is to meditate. I don't mean you have to get all weird, let your hair grow long, and join a commune. I mean you need to learn how to get in tune with yourself and start to refine your product by spending time developing your brain. Learn how you are feeling in your own shoes, and then you will be able to figure out how to put yourself in your customer's shoes. By doing so, you may even figure out how to make a new shoe!

No Pain, No Gain

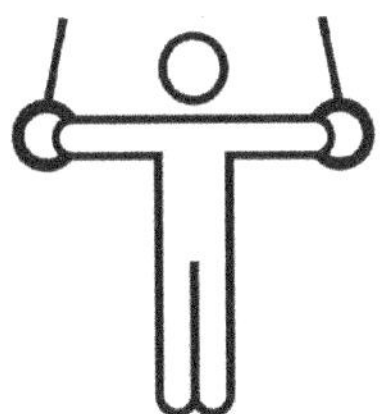

Training your brain to learn how to serve everyone like a customer takes work. You are in essence trying to rewire your brain. But you can change your focus immediately and start the process of modifying your thinking. All you need to do is to start learning how to understand your feelings toward events or people.

By understanding yourself first, you will be able to understand how others might be feeling. Once you understand yourself and how others might feel based on your perspective, you can start to imagine how others may react based on their perspective. When you're able to understand people based on their perspective, you will be in a position to serve everyone like a customer every time, all the time. You will have empathy.

A study conducted by Harvard University found that the best salespeople in the world have a high degree of empathy[85]. They are able to use their empathy to get into the minds of their customers to determine and anticipate their most important needs. This skill

[85] (Ruth, Wysocki, Farnsworth, & Clark, n.d.)

helps salespeople focus on serving their customers' most important needs, which in turn helps them to win new business.

The best salespeople often develop their empathy from personal experience. They acquire empathy for customers by working in the same field or through self-education. This helps the salesperson gain firsthand experience and insight into the customer's perspective. With such a perspective, a salesperson is able to empathize and serve needs better than his competitor does.

You have to go native.

Remember that I said you can't have a dual value system when you serve your customers. You need to serve everyone like a customer to build your empathy skills.

If you try to maintain a dual value system, you'll slip up just as Stan did and miss an opportunity. More importantly, you will weaken your mind if you're choosy about whom you serve like a customer.

Also, what does a dual value system say about your character?

You have to apply the system all the time to everyone without regard for their status, title, and position. When you do this, you strengthen your mind's ability to be empathetic. The result is that you'll constantly be thinking about ways to serve customers. In this state of mind, you'll find new ways to sell your product or service and identify new products and services to sell. This will lead you to new and important life-changing ideas that, if cultivated and developed, will help you achieve success. Of course, you can spend time thinking about making money, but doing that probably won't get you anywhere because your focus is not on the person or people who will give you money.

Your job is to do everything you can to be empathetic and serve everyone like a customer, without judgment, favor, or distinction. You're trying to train yourself to reshape your mind, and achieve all of your dreams. All of that requires total dedication and commitment. Weekend warriors need not apply.

Service Starts at the Top

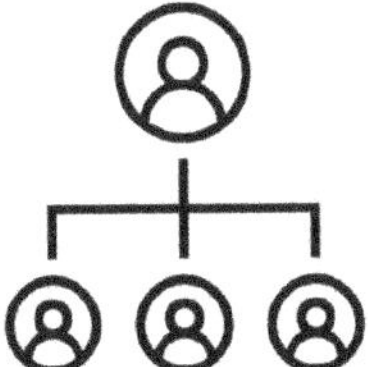

I often hear corporate executives talk about the need to be more customer focused. Of course, I couldn't agree more. Yet having a customer orientation is not something that comes naturally to all individuals, let alone an entire corporation of hundreds or thousands of employees. As we've just seen, learning to be empathetic to all customers all the time takes practice and work. Trying to get all employees to reorient their mind and serve everyone like a customer is a bit like trying to herd cats. Yet, if you don't figure out how to get everyone to readjust how they think, then you'll never really figure out how to become customer oriented.

I think of an organization like a brain and employees like little neurons running around communicating messages. In a healthy organization, the employees work well together, and the flow of information is efficient and effective. As one employee receives vital information, the other carries it to key decision makers. These decision makers then help the organization respond, the same way our central nervous system responds when we feel pleasure or pain.

In unhealthy organizations, the opposite is true. In such companies many of the important "neurons" (i.e., employees) are not well connected and are underdeveloped. Inside these companies, employees display a lack of empathy towards one another and they are reluctant to share information. More importantly, they have few if any vehicles to collect and share information about the customer and even less understanding of how to use it. These organizations have the darndest time trying to grow sales because customer service isn't part of the corporate DNA.

Service starts at the top of the organization, not the bottom, assuming that you believe a bottom exists. Company leaders must serve their employees to establish a culture of service. Employees need to be cared for, praised, and compensated very well. Research shows that when you serve your employees this way, productivity surges, and customer satisfaction increases.

We can't get away with saying we're customer focused. We have to practice our philosophy by serving everyone like a customer all the time.

Chapter 11

Billionaire Vision

The most successful people got that way because they saw an opportunity where others didn't. In fact, one of the richest women in the world built her fortune from trash.

Yes, trash.

In 1985, Zhang Yin lost her job as an accountant for a Chinese trading company in Hong Kong. Yin was offered a job at a different company that would pay her $64,000 a year (a lot of money at the time), but she declined it. She identified a better opportunity awaiting her if she ventured out on her own.

Yin had noticed that Chinese companies didn't have enough cardboard to support their burgeoning export business, while the U.S. seemed to be buried in wastepaper. With just $4,000, she started her own company to buy wastepaper from U.S. intermediaries and then ship it to China. She then turned the wastepaper into cardboard for use in Chinese exports.

In 1990, Yin moved to Los Angeles and bought wastepaper directly from garbage dumps, who gave it to her cheap, since they were happy to get rid of it. She also found that cargo ships from China often returned home from the U.S. empty, and they were willing to ship Yin's wastepaper back to China for minimal expense. These cost dynamics and market dynamics that Yin discovered turned her into a billionaire.

Yin said she saw a forest of trees where others saw garbage[86]. You too, can find such opportunities when you really look for ways to better serve customers.

While such opportunities abound, they are not always easy to find. I can't emphasize this point enough. We need to train ourselves how to look closely, and then we need to know what to look for to find opportunities.

You are going to need a framework to help you spot customer needs.

Every person has four types of basic needs.

The first type is physical. Physical needs are things we need to survive. Food and water are good examples. You can't live without them.

The second type of need is functional. These needs help us accomplish an important task. They are usually a means to an end. A hammer serves a functional need. We don't buy a hammer just for the sake of it. We buy it to pound nails.

The third type of need serves people's emotions. Serving emotional needs makes people feel good. For example, you can serve somebody's emotional need by giving them a compliment. By doing so, you will serve a person's need for esteem.

The fourth type of need serves our intellect. Intellectual needs are derived from our values. An example might be the need to be creative or to be healthy. You don't usually wake up and decide you want to be creative or healthy.

---

86 (Barboza, 2007)

These needs develop naturally from our interests, experiences, or complex thoughts about what's important in life.

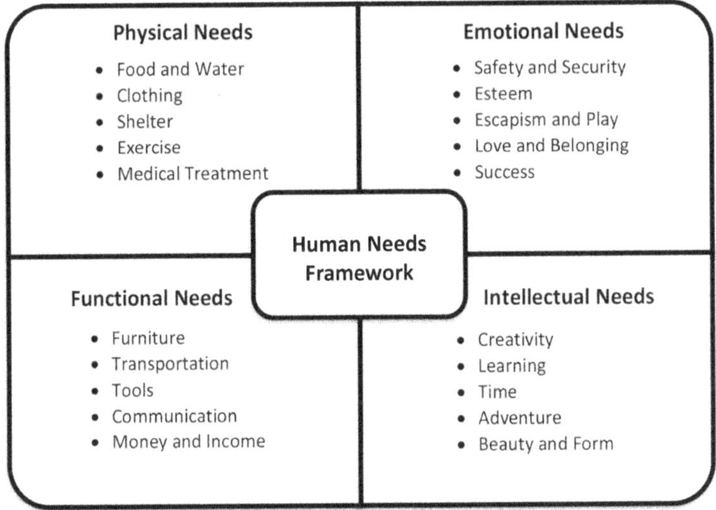

Think about industries that serve the physical need to eat and get basic sustenance. The grocery business serves this need, and it generates around $682.8 billion a year[87]. If you serve customers' basic physical needs, you might be able to capture some of this wealth.

If you are like me, you probably like to go to the movies once in a while. Movie theaters serve our emotional need for escapism. The U.S. movie business generates about $11.3 billion annually by serving this simple need[88].

What about intellectual needs? We all have them. Many of us have intellectual needs for beauty, form, and refinement. U.S. art dealers and galleries cater to this need, which is a $9 billion market[89].

87 (Grocery store sales in the United States from 1992 to 2019, n.d.)

88 (Domestic Movie Theatrical Market Summary 1995 to 2020, n.d.)

89 (Art Dealers in the US industry statistics, n.d.)

Most of the products we buy and own are functional in nature, right? Think of your cell phone. It functions to help you communicate with people who are not in your immediate vicinity. The U.S. wireless telecommunication industry serves this need and generates $190 billion annually by doing so. That's one big cell phone bill!

The four need types are not independent from one another. With the exception of the most primitive societies, our needs aren't always met in isolation or sequence, and they aren't always one-dimensional, either, because we are not one-dimensional.

You can often find ways to serve multiple needs simultaneously in unique ways.

For instance, the physical need for water and the emotional need for esteem can be tied together to nourish a person's body and mind. Companies like VOSS water are a good example.

VOSS has been able to package, price, and promote their water as an upscale brand. If people see you with a bottle of VOSS water, you get a bit of esteem, so consumers are happy to pay a premium price for it. The market for bottled water is a $61 billion market in the United States[90]. That's a lot of water!

Interaction of Physical and Emotional Needs

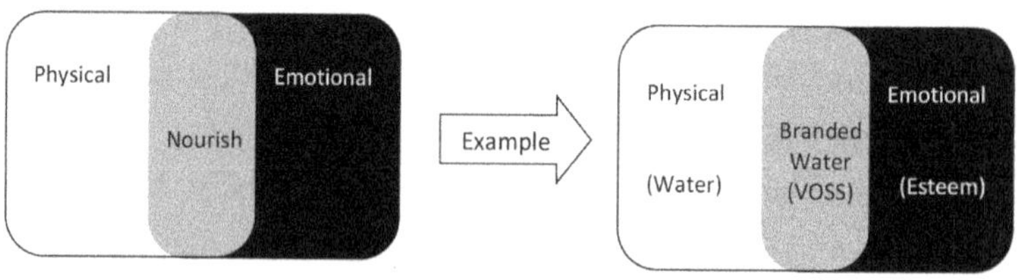

You might think that branded water is a waste of money. If you are only concerned with the physical need for hydration, you'd

[90] (Bottled Water, n.d.)

be correct. However, people desire esteem. If for a few extra dollars people can get a taste of it, they will pay for it. Do you see anything wrong with that? I don't. We all have different needs.

Many other interesting need interactions exist that savvy people have stumbled upon. Take the functional need to communicate and the emotional need to belong. What might this create? How about social networking?

Facebook, the leading social networking site, has achieved a meteoric rise from a few hundred thousand college student users to more than 2.6 billion. How? It tapped an unmet need to stay connected and enjoy a sense of belonging.

Facebook is a pretty simple idea, but until recently, nobody had thought of it.

But when Facebook came on the scene, almost everyone understood the value of it immediately. After about 13 years of service, Facebook is now valued as a multibillion-dollar company.

Interaction of Functional and Emotional Needs

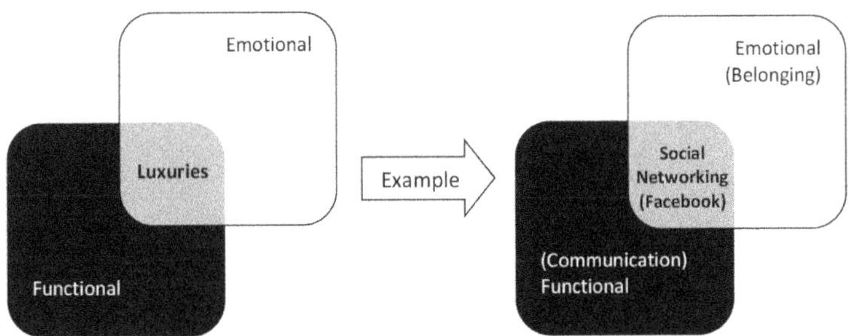

You will find a couple of additional two-dimensional need combinations below that you'll recognize. These combinations are meant to give you some examples of how needs can interact, along with the solutions that were created to serve those need interactions.

Interaction of Other Human Needs

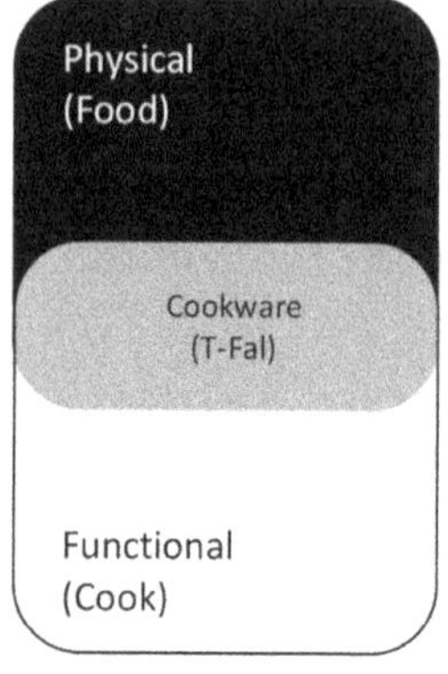

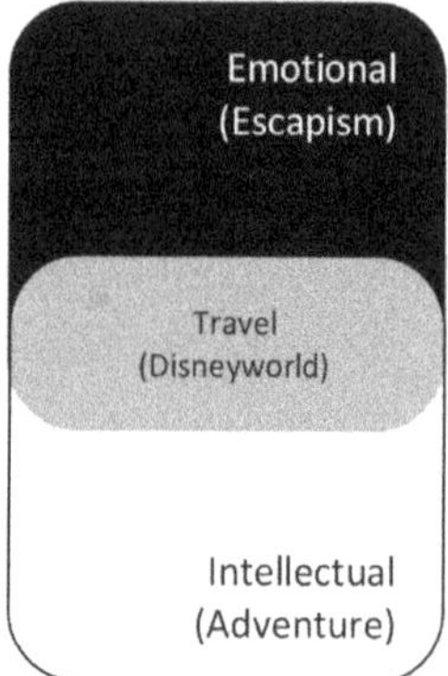

Can you think of any other need combinations?

If you can, you might have discovered a new opportunity to serve your customers. The reality is that many need combination possibilities exist—some which have yet to be discovered. Yet they can all be illustrated in a single construct named Human Need Theorem.

Human Needs Theorem

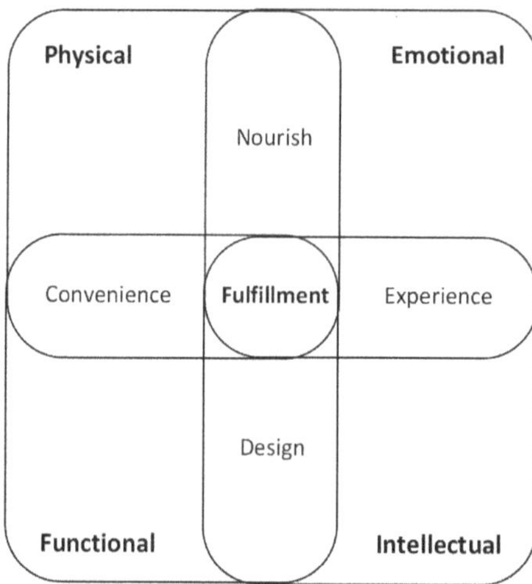

The Human Need Theorem, shown above, depicts the interaction possibilities of the four need types. For instance, when any of the four need types intersect, that creates another need type which is represented here in the area that overlaps. I show only some of the possibilities above. Many others exist and are yet to be discovered.

This construct reconciles the phenomenon we see in our own personal desires. We need food and water, but as our needs mature, we also need conveniences; hence, the value of bottled water.

The best services and products aren't one-dimensional. They serve multiple needs. Consider energy drinks. They serve the physical need for hydration along with the intellectual need for alertness. Branded energy drinks also serve our need for esteem (e.g., we can drink a RockStar!), and they are easy to buy and consume. Is it any wonder that the U.S. market for energy drinks is about $18 billion annually?

Your challenge and opportunity are to discover a new combination of needs to serve your customers. You will have to work at it, but if you stay focused on connecting needs in new and exciting ways, you can achieve The Hidden Fortune of Service.

Try to solve the biggest problems for your customers. You don't want to spend all your time and energy solving the smallest problems because they will bring you only small rewards. Instead, find big problems to solve because those will be your best opportunities.

Understanding the Needs of Business Customers

Just like consumers, businesspeople and employees have needs. Their needs typically concern doing their job well or surviving in their job. They are focused on climbing the corporate ladder to greater income.

Each employee has a specific job function in their company. Their job function could be working in customer service, sales, marketing, operations (e.g., like a shipping and receiving clerk), accounting, and food service (e.g., a chef). Everyone has some kind of job function. Each job function has specific needs required to perform that job. The needs can be broken down into responsibilities, processes, tasks, and materials[91]. The Corporate Needs Ladder below illustrates needs and the relative importance of each one.

The Corporate Needs Ladder

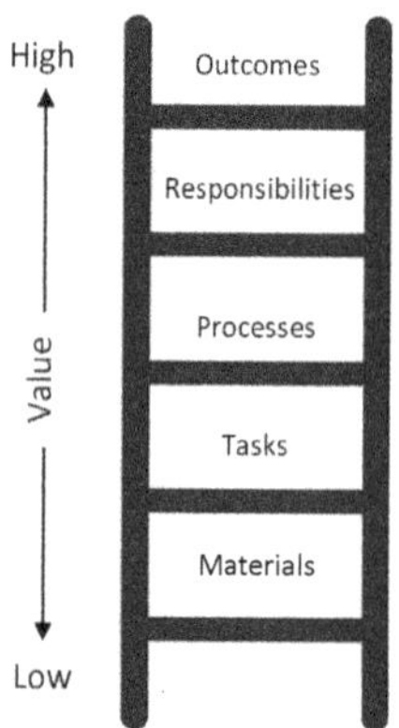

Outcomes: Represent the business results a person wants to achieve that are specific to their job function (e.g. revenue, earnings, net income, ROI, etc.

Responsibilities: The things a person is responsible to do as part of their job function (e.g. cook hamburgers)

Processes: Like a complete food recipe, used to complete a job responsibility (e.g. shape hamburger, place on pan, cook at certain temperature, etc.)

Tasks: steps in a food recipe (e.g. cook hamburger to an internal temperature of 160 degrees)

Materials: The raw ingredients needed to accomplish a task, complete a process or full responsibilities (e.g. hamburger meat, buns, etc.)

The higher you climb in your service offering, the more value you provide to your business customer. If, for instance, you serve an employee's need to drive an outcome, you provide far more value than supplying materials for them to do their job. If you help them with one of their job responsibilities, that is more valuable than helping them with a job task.

91

You might think that the highest rung of the ladder is the most important. This isn't true. The highest rung depends on the lowest rung. This dependency suggests that the best services will help your customers climb higher.

Every rung on the ladder is a business opportunity for you to offer a service.

For instance, take the top rung. Many companies exist to help businesspeople achieve their targeted business outcomes. Companies in the consulting business such as McKinsey, Bain, Boston Consulting Group, and Accenture all fit this profile.

A *consultant* focuses on providing strategies that will improve the odds of achieving a business outcome, and businesspeople pay them a lot of money for this. In fact, the U.S. consulting business is a $251 billion-dollar-a-year business.[92] Perhaps you could think of a new consulting business.

Your service can start and stop anywhere on The Corporate Needs Ladder.

As another example, companies that make software often try to automate various tasks to increase productivity. Many companies buy software because of the business benefits (outcomes) that software promises (saving money). According to Hoovers, the U.S. software development market generates $285 billion dollars a year[93].

You can choose to offer materials only. Many successful companies start and stop at this rung. However, you should always consider the ultimate value of your service offering in terms of the outcomes it produces. Research shows that this will improve sales and customer satisfaction.

---

92 (Management Consulting in the US industry statistics, n.d.)

93 (Estimated revenue of U.S. software publishers from 2005 to 2019, n.d.)

Building Your Perspective on Customers and Their Needs

We have reviewed many different ways to look at your customers, whether they're a consumer or a business. Each perspective will help you understand the needs of the customers you are serving and help you gain more specific insights about their requirements. The more specific you are in profiling your customers, the easier it will be to serve their needs.

In fact, if you can learn to serve everyone uniquely, based on their specific needs, you will develop superior service.

Dell Computer is perhaps one of the best-known examples of serving everyone like a customer. They will configure and sell you a computer based on your unique needs. They have perfected mass customization. As a result, in just twenty-seven years Dell has increased sales from zero to $64 billion.

You can attain The Hidden Fortune of Service when you serve everyone like a customer as uniquely as possible.

Chapter 12

Two Questions for the Great Ones

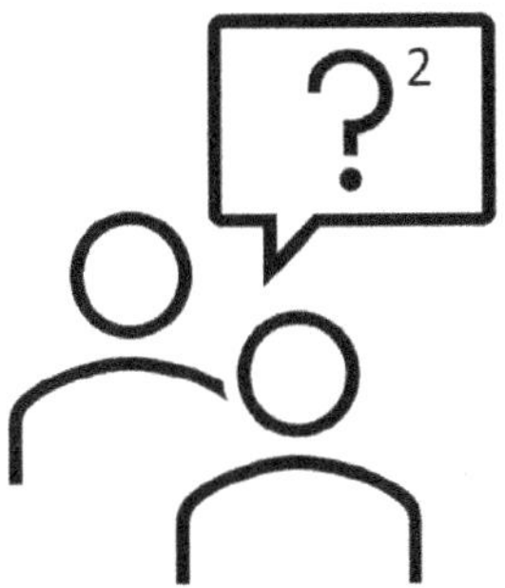

Have you seen a dream car you'd like to own?

If so, you may have gone so far as to do some research on it. Someday, you think, I will get that car.

My dream car is an Audi R8 GT Coupe. Have you ever seen one? If not, look it up. It's an amazing car.

One day I was driving down the street when I saw a guy driving one. I wondered what he did for a living. I mean, an Audi R8 GT isn't exactly a mid-priced vehicle.

It can cost about $200,000. A car that expensive would require a monthly payment of $4,000 with nothing down, at an interest rate of around six percent. This is assuming that someone who could afford an Audi R8 would actually choose to finance it.

I started to think about what a person would have to earn to afford a car loan of that amount. I figured this person made about $60,000 a month or about $720,000 a year. I was curious about what this man did for a living. I wanted to stop and ask him, but I just kept driving.

I made a terrible mistake. Studying the competition can often help you gain insights in order to improve your product which would have taken many years to do if you had to do surveys and learn on your own. While I knew this fact in my professional career, it never occurred to me to think about how this would benefit me personally. Don't make the same mistake. Study the competition because doing so will help accelerate your success.

If you haven't seen the movie *The Pursuit of Happyness*, rent it. It's based on a true story about Chris Gardner, a struggling salesman and single parent who found himself homeless while trying to raise his baby boy. During a low point in Gardner's life, he met a wealthy man who drove a red Ferrari.

Curious, Gardner mustered up the nerve to ask the man two questions that changed his life: "What do you do?" and "How do you do that[94]?" The man with the red Ferrari was a stockbroker, and as a result, that's what Chris Gardner set out to become.

With no education or connections, he worked hard to break into the industry and finally got an opportunity with Dean Witter. He had to start out by making cold calls to prospective clients, but he got results immediately. His road to success wasn't without its challenges, however.

One of his clients assumed Gardner was white and would tell him all kinds of off-color racial jokes over the phone before he asked Gardner to place a trade for whatever shares Gardner was promoting. Gardner, who is black, kept his peace and continued to serve that client by making him a lot of money.

When the client set out to meet the person who was making him so much money, Gardner said he thought that his customer

---

94 (chrisgardnermedia.com, n.d.)

would either pull all of his money from the firm or give Gardner all his money to invest. After meeting Gardner, the client gave him all his money to invest. Twenty years and many customers later, Chris Gardner became a multimillionaire.

You can accelerate your success in life if you do as Chris Gardner did. Study successful people, companies, and products. Learn what they do and how they do it. Then go out and do the same thing, and you'll get the same results.

Studying the competition is something that most successful people do, and it is often the only way to be successful. Consider the field of Law.

Lawyers study the competition by reviewing those who have successfully argued similar cases. As lawyers prepare for trial, they spend much of their time reviewing legal cases similar to the charges they are opposing or prosecuting. If the body of case law supports the lawyer's argument for or against the charge, it's called *precedence*. Precedence can give a lawyer a substantial advantage if s/he can find at least one precedent.

The success of others should be *your* precedent, as well. Study their process and ask them the *essential two* questions that Gardner used.

Chapter 13

Give Yourself a SWOT

Strengths. Weaknesses. Opportunities. Threats.

That's what *SWOT* stands for in the business world. You may have heard that acronym before, but if you haven't, it's about time you did.

Businesses spend a lot of time and money trying to figure out their SWOT based on feedback from internal and external sources. SWOT is such a critical aspect of business planning that you will find that almost every business plan contains one, and it is often updated annually, if not more often. It isn't easy work, but it is critical for a business.

Billion-dollar businesses use a SWOT to determine how best to pursue their objectives for making money and improving customer satisfaction. Doesn't it make sense that the same techniques can help you do the same?

Do yourself a favor and take a lesson from those who have already achieved great success. Take a good SWOT at yourself. You can't hope to become successful if you don't.

The best way to think of a SWOT is as a personal self-assessment. During the first part of the SWOT assessment, you should gather external information about your *strengths* and *weaknesses*. The second part of the SWOT involves an assessment of external *opportunities* and *threats*.

Apply the Techniques of Big Business: SWOT Yourself

Before we do a SWOT analysis on you, you'll need to define an objective for yourself. You and I will have a hard time trying to figure out your strengths and weaknesses if we don't have the proper context.

For example, if you want to be a millionaire, you will have certain strengths and weaknesses that pertain to that objective. Developing a clear objective for yourself is the starting point for preparing your SWOT.

You might believe that writing personal objectives should be easy. How hard can it be to write an objective that says you want to be successful? All you have to do is jot down something like, "I want to make a million dollars," right? The problem with objectives like this is that they aren't very clear.

If your objective is to make a million dollars, you may get your wish with little effort. Consider that the average annual household income in the U.S. is about $50,000 a year. If you work for twenty years, you will make a million dollars. You might tell me, "That's not what I meant."

My response to you is, "So what did you mean? You said you wanted to make a million dollars, and you likely will, over a lifetime." What you probably meant is that you want to make a million dollars next year or much sooner. But when exactly next year do you want to make a million dollars? You need to be specific.

A good objective statement will be specific, measurable, action-oriented, realistic, and time-bound (SMART). Be as specific as you can be about your objective. Saying you want to be successful doesn't tell me much, and it doesn't tell you much, either. More importantly, achieving success is difficult to do when you aren't exactly sure what *success* means. So, if you can start your SWOT by outlining what you want to achieve, you'll be much more likely to achieve it.

If you want to achieve The Hidden Fortune of Service, make the customer the centerpiece of your objective. Describe the customers you will serve and what you expect to achieve by doing that.

Once you determine specifically whom you want to serve and what you want to achieve, the next step is to figure out how to *measure* whether you achieved it.

For instance, if you tell me you want to sell a new service to customers, then you will need to identify how many customers you want to buy from you.

An objective statement should also be action oriented. An action-oriented objective is written with an action verb instead of a state-of-being verb. This means the subject in the sentence, probably you, should be doing something.

Objectives should be *realistic* without giving up the dream. I believe you will achieve what you set out to do as long as your primary focus is to better serve your customers. So, make the customer part of your objective.

The final aspect of writing SMART goals is to make sure they are time-bound, or time-sensitive. You should think of *time-bound objectives* as ones that have a set date for achievement. For example, if you want to increase your income by fifty percent, you should set a date for when you will achieve it.

You might think it is odd to detail your objectives when you haven't a clue whether you will be able to achieve them. The first step in planning is not to determine *how* you will do it but *what* you want to do. Don't sabotage yourself before you get started because you might be tempted to find countless reasons why you can't achieve your objective. Instead, *think like* big business. First decide what you want to achieve, then figure out how to get there.

Developing Your SWOT

The matrix below provides a structure and a definition for each aspect of the SWOT. This is what the most successful companies use to determine how best to achieve their objective. We'll discuss each aspect of the matrix in detail.

Objective: Increase my income fifty percent in the next year by offering my customers a better mousetrap.

SWOT Matrix[95]

	Strengths	**Weaknesses**
Internal	Internal attributes or qualities that will help you achieve your objective.	Internal shortcomings or handicaps that will make it harder for you to achieve your objective.
	Opportunities	**Threats**
External	External factors or circumstances that will help you achieve your objective.	External factors or circumstances that will make it harder for you to achieve your objective.

95 (Kotler & Armstrong, 2008)

Know Your Strengths

Your strengths are the internal attributes or qualities that will help you achieve your objective. You most likely have more strengths than you realize, and for this reason, you may find it hard to determine your strengths on your own. You will need the help of your customers to determine your strengths.

At one time or another, your customers may have praised you about something you did. Such praise is worth noting. If other people have given you similar praise, you may have a natural talent you didn't know you had.

Our talents are almost always hidden until we are in the service of our customers. Through our service, we can discover what we are good at. The more service we provide, the more talents we find and the more strengths we identify.

You can ask your customers for feedback when you want to identify your strengths. This is one of the best methods for identifying what you are good at.

Sometimes you may find yourself in a situation where your customers have never praised you. Worse, you may be in a situation where they constantly point out all of your faults. Whatever the case, you can find other ways to identify your strengths without direct compliments from your customers.

For instance, we know when the marketplace likes something regardless if the customer tells us or not. How? They vote with their dollars. That is, if customers like it, they buy it. The same principle holds true in all things. If people like what you do, they will keep you around.

Know Your Weaknesses

Some of us don't want to admit we have weaknesses. Weaknesses are certainly nothing to celebrate, but they aren't something to be afraid of. They are just weaknesses.

Businesses focus on collecting facts about weaknesses. They *try* to stay dispassionate about what they find. But once businesspeople find a weakness, they focus on correcting it.

Think like a businessman. Identify your weaknesses and then determine how to fix them.

Just as you asked your customers for feedback on your strengths, so, too, will you need to turn to your customers for feedback about your weaknesses. If you leveraged the techniques in the chapter on customer research, then you have probably identified your weaknesses already.

Whatever your weakness may be, make sure that you state only the weaknesses that are pertinent to the objective at hand. Any weakness you identify should be a requirement for achieving the objective.

For instance, if you want a new job and you don't have the required education, then that's a weakness in your candidacy.

Why?

Education is a prerequisite.

Once you know your weaknesses, you can focus your attention on how to mitigate them.

Know Your Opportunities

Opportunities are those things that you will be able to use in order to get ahead. For example, let's suppose your objective is to start a new business to provide services for other businesses. An *opportunity* might be a new loan program sponsored by the government. This would be an opportunity because it was created by something or someone else, and it supports your objective.

Great opportunities abound in your life, but you have to work at it to truly see them because they are often difficult to detect. In fact, a key difference between the most successful and least successful people is the ability to see opportunities and seize them.

Know Your Threats

Threats are external factors or influences that will make it harder for you to achieve your objective. If you pay attention and do your research, you will find many threats to achieving your objective of better serving your customers.

Businesses are confronted by threats to their success, but they cannot always see them coming. A good example of such threats is the impact of digital photography on the sales of 35mm film.

The digital camera represents a significant innovation that has given people many more possibilities for sharing pictures. This was especially important because the advent of the Internet and email has made user-generated content a phenomenon in just ten short years.

In 1999, eight hundred million rolls of 35mm film were sold. By 2006, that number had declined to 204 million[96]. In just five years, the unit volume of 35mm film sales dropped by almost seventy-five percent. Stay out of that business!

In 2009, Kodak announced that it would discontinue one of its flagship film brands, Kodachrome, citing declining sales[97]. Kodak has since struggled to adapt to the digital camera revolution because it suffered from the inertia of success. They never saw the threat coming until it was too late. They weren't able to react quickly enough, and as a result, they suffered from plummeting sales and earnings.

Threats can suddenly appear if you aren't keeping an eye out for them.

Don't be a victim of carelessness. Beware of the threats that could destroy your ability to achieve your objective of serving your customer.

---

96 (Hafner, 2007)

97 (Kodak kills Kodachrome film after 74 years, n.d.)

Putting Your SWOT Together

We have reviewed the four areas of the SWOT. Now it's time to put it all together. As an example, the objective and SWOT shown below were drafted for a person who wants to increase their income by fifty percent. Notice that the strengths and weaknesses all begin with you. The opportunities and threats are all external and all focus on the customer, to keep the example simple.

Objective: Increase my income fifty percent in the next year serving by building and selling a better mousetrap.

SWOT Matrix[98]

	Strengths	**Weaknesses**
Internal	• You have good sales skills • You have a good product idea	• You don't have a lot of customers • You don't have money to build the product
	Opportunities	**Threats**
External	• Gov't will guarantee a loan for you • Customers have a need for product	• Competitors offer a similar product • Gov't is evaluating the safety of idea

After reviewing this SWOT, you may have some ideas about how this person could achieve the objective. That's exactly what happens when you develop a good SWOT: You get ideas about how to achieve your objective. You have focus and direction on what you need to do to make things happen. You're empowered to make the right type of changes to better serve your customers.

98

Chapter 14

The "You" Brand

When I was growing up, I would listen to the radio for hours on end. When I heard a song I really liked, I would go to a music store to buy it.

Buying it wasn't always easy. I often had the hardest time trying to figure out the name of the song or the band, because radio stations—at the least the ones I listened to—weren't very good about identifying the song or the artist and the Shazam app didn't exist back then. Consequently, I would try to sing the song I heard to the store clerk to see if he could figure it out. It was a real hoot, literally. The clerk would look at me as though I needed professional help or at minimum some singing lessons.

One of the unintended consequences of my hit-and-run singing was that store clerks branded me as "the loony tune." I was known as the walk-in bozo who required a new level of customer service—one that required the clerk to name that tune. That is not the reputation one wants to carry around, but that's what happens when you aren't careful about managing your personal brand image. I branded myself, just as a product does. But in my case, I did it by accident, and I did a terrible job.

Whether you like it or not, you have developed a type of brand image in the minds of your customers. Maybe you're known for being aggressive or smart, or maybe others think you are a total jerk. Whatever it may be, you have a personal brand image, and it is real. You have to live with it or learn how to change it.

There is an old saying that a good name is better than precious ointment; better than great riches; to be esteemed over silver and gold. Why?

A good reputation solicits favor, wins support, and helps you advance in life and business.

If your brand reputation is working for you, people will search you out. If you continue to deliver the goods, your good reputation will continue to grow. But if you have a bad brand reputation, that's going to make life more difficult.

If you have a bad brand, then you may want to do something about it. In the business world, marketers often resort to advertising and public relations campaigns to try to change their brand image. These campaigns often cost millions of dollars and often fail to achieve the desired effect. Why? Customers don't believe a brand changed just because someone told them it did. Businesses have to prove the product change if they want to win back customers.

I often tell the management I work with that the best marketing in the world is having the best product. A good product will get more marketing buzz and word of mouth than any marketing campaign could ever hope to generate. The same goes for you. If you deliver great results, others will notice, and word will get around. The "You Brand" will develop value and meaning. But what will that reputation be? Is it the reputation you want?

Developing Your Brand

Most people don't manage their personal brand because they don't think of themselves as a product. But you *are* a product. You, as the product, have also built a reputation, and that reputation is your brand. Your brand may be something good, or it may be something bad, but you have a brand.

If you want to change your brand, you will have to work at establishing a new brand identity for yourself. The leading branding experts will tell you that a good brand identity has four dimensions: the product itself, brand personality, brand symbols, and brand affiliations. These same four dimensions are just as applicable to you as they are to anything you might find on a store shelf.

You're the Product

Defining your personal product brand means you need to identify the attributes you want to magnify and be known for by your customers. Perhaps you want to be known as a problem solver, innovator, confidant, or expert or as someone who is knowledgeable, able to deliver results, educated, or physically beautiful. Whatever attributes you decide on, make sure they are ones your customers really care about. And make sure you don't try to turn yourself into something you don't want to be.

Avoid changing the essence of your personal brand every time a customer asks you to do so. Remember that a good product is comprised of ingredients that make it unique and something that customers can count on when they need it. If you constantly change to cater to every customer's request, you'll be defined as an *all-purpose* product, and those typically don't do very well. Decide which attributes you want to be known for and then exemplify them to better serve your customers.

Be careful not to fall prey to "Occupational Irony." *Occupational Irony* is a principle that states some people in an occupation are often unable to serve themselves the same way they serve others. Examples are an outstanding financial advisor who can't manage his finances, or the marketing person who can promote anything but can't manage his personal brand.

The danger of falling victim to Occupational Irony is that you weaken your personal brand. If you are unable to do for yourself the same things you propose to do for others, customers may question your abilities. The best way to avoid the trap is to demonstrate you, as the product, can deliver value for yourself.

Build Your Brand Personality

As you practice managing your brand as a product, you also need to think about *your brand personality.* Your brand personality is determined by characteristics you exhibit when you do something. If you smile and are friendly when you deliver your product, people will conclude that you must be nice and friendly.

If you are angry and short with people, they will assume that your brand personality is rude, mean, or unfriendly.

However you decide to deliver your product, remember that you are creating a brand personality for yourself with every interaction you have with your customers. This means that the method of delivering your product is just as important as the product itself. How you do something is just as important as what you do.

Instead of reacting differently to each situation you encounter, decide what kind of brand personality you want to be known for so that you behave accordingly, regardless of the situation.

Generally speaking, people like to be around other people who are friendly, outgoing, attractive, intelligent, successful, witty, compassionate, and interesting. Conversely, people avoid others who are angry, mean, unkempt, ignorant, rude, unsympathetic, violent, and boring.

Is your brand personality going to be one that people want to have around or one that people want to avoid? If your brand personality is one that people want to avoid, then you will become akin to a toilet bowl brush—a necessary evil but good only for the dirtiest of jobs.

Don't get flushed!

The Law of Scarcity

Before you overwhelm the world with your new brand personality, you must be aware of the Law of Scarcity and its ability to help you or hurt you.

The Law of Scarcity is an economic principle that states that when something of value is in limited supply, the perceived value of it increases, causing demand to increase. This means the less of something there is, the more it's valued.

If your customers think you are too easy to access, the Law of Scarcity may work against you, causing your perceived value to decrease. In fact, you may even wear out your welcome and cause people to avoid you. You have to manage how much of your product (you) customers can get so that you always keep them coming back for more. To some degree, you need to play hard to get.

Create Your Brand Symbols

Part of good branding is having a *brand symbol* (Aaker, 1996). A brand symbol can be anything, but it's a distinctive reminder of the particular quality, style, and value of the product it represents. Interestingly, the scarcer a product is, the more revered the brand symbol becomes.

Some good examples of this is the Mercedes-Benz three-pointed star. This symbol was meant to represent the founder's goal of universal motorization on land, on water, and in the air[99]. When the founder's sons became executives of the company,

[99] (Ernst, n.d.)

they made the three-pointed star the official logo. The logo is a reminder of the personal triumph of a man who told his wife that one day his star would shine over his own factory to symbolize prosperity. Indeed, the star still shines brightly.

You need to develop your own brand symbol to make yourself distinctive and memorable. Your brand symbol should be something that you use regularly, is distinctive, and is not overbearing. It might be a style of dress, a signature, a hairstyle, a type of glasses, or something else.

Many famous celebrities, musicians, and famous business people have successfully used brand symbols for themselves. Think of Donald Trump, now The President of the United States. He has used his last name as a symbol for a number of different businesses and products. He even has a nickname— "the Donald." Regardless of what you think of his politics, he's a pretty amazing marketer.

Pick Your Affiliations

The last aspect of your brand identity is the brand affiliations you make for yourself. Your brand affiliations are the organizations and people you chose to associate with your brand. An example of a brand affiliation might be the religious organization you frequent, the volunteer organization you support, the country club you become a member of, or the successful people you golf with on Saturdays. These organizations and people rub off some of their brand identity on you. This is great if these people have a positive image. But if they have a negative image, they may weaken your brand image.

You are known by the friends you keep. As such, it is best for you to decide how you want to be known, find people or organizations that support your brand identity, and then make an effort to affiliate with them.

You also need to reexamine the people and organizations you currently affiliate with to determine if they are appropriate for your newly fashioned brand identity.

If they are not, you will need to disassociate yourself from them.

Define Your Brand Value Proposition

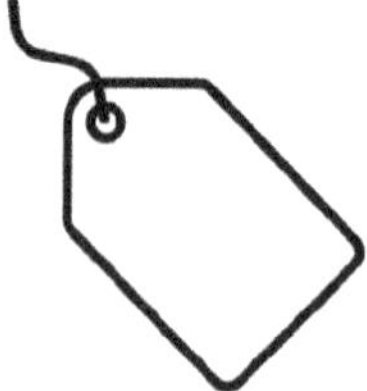

The last point in building your personal brand is about your value proposition. If you've ever interviewed for a job, you've probably had to answer a question like, "Why should I hire you?"

That's difficult to answer because to do so correctly you have to know what's really important to the hiring manager. Then you have to demonstrate that you're the best one or maybe the only one who can deliver the goods. If a person can't demonstrate superior value, he won't get the job.

Your customers are asking themselves the same kind of questions about you. Some might be thinking, "Why should I keep you?" Others might think, "Why should I love you?" Still others might be wondering, "Why should I buy from you?"

You have to be able to answer these questions before your customers ask them. We must constantly demonstrate our value in words, actions, and deeds if we are to be successful. We need to have a *strong value proposition.*

Your personal brand value proposition is the value you propose to your customers as a product.

The value you propose should be more than enough to persuade people to keep you around. In fact, your value proposition has to be compelling if you want your customers to keep coming back for more.

The most successful businesses in the world work very hard to develop their value proposition. They understand that if they are to find and keep a customer happy, then they have to provide real value. If they fail to provide value, they lose customers. This applies to you as well. You have to know your value, and you have to be able to communicate it if you want to keep your customers or find new ones.

Chapter 15

Talk Your Way In

The other day my daughter and I were walking in the park when she said to me, "Dad, what's an aunt sister?"

"An aunt sister?" I asked.

"Yes," she replied.

I was stumped. How can a woman be both an aunt and a sister? I concluded that a father and his daughter would have to have a child together in order for the child to have an aunt sister. Yuck! But that was the answer, so I told her that.

Silly me.

"Is that what my teacher means when she asks about my aunt sisters?" my daughter asked.

Pause.

She meant *ancestor*, not *aunt sister*!

"Oh . . . sorry, honey. Daddy misunderstood you. Um, no, our an-ces-tors are German, Italian, Jewish and Indian."

How did I miss that one?

Too funny.

We were talking past each other. My daughter couldn't enunciate the word *ancestor* correctly, so I had misinterpreted what she meant. In order to make sense of her question, I had to consider her age, her education, her abilities, and even the question her teacher asked.

If you are going to serve your customer, you will also need to consider where people are coming from—what they are really saying. We need to be cognizant of intercultural differences.

Me vs. We

Culture can be described as a set of shared beliefs, attitudes, and practices shared by a group of people.

A culture can be individualistic or collectivistic[100].

You can think of an *individualistic culture* as one that celebrates the individual and teaches the importance of personal responsibility. Most *collectivistic cultures* stress the importance of the society, community, and family instead of the individual.

Most Asian cultures are collectivist, meaning they tend to think in terms of "we" or "us" when making decisions. This cultural orientation is so strong it has been used to persuade people to give up their own life.

---

[100] (Gudykunst & Kim, 1997)

During World War II, the Japanese military exploited collectivist values to persuade pilots to give their life for their country by crashing their plane into enemy targets. These men became known as "kamikazes" literally translated as "divine wind"[101]. During recruitment, the Japanese military discovered they often had more volunteers than planes.

European cultures are more individualistic, so they tend to think more in terms of "me" or "I." An individualistic culture encourages people to pursue their personal dreams, goals, and ambitions. These cultures celebrate personal achievements far more than teams, groups, or companies do.

A person's cultural orientation toward collectivism or individualism can affect how they perceive the world and events[102]. In one research study, people from Western and Eastern cultures were given a picture to study and then asked questions about it after it was taken from them. Westerners were more apt to remember the central character of the picture, while people from Eastern cultures were more likely to remember details of the scene's background.

These findings and those of other studies prove that the Western mind is conditioned to think about individuals, whereas Easterners are more likely to think about communities or the larger environment. Such an orientation seems trivial until you realize that trying to serve the needs of your customer may require you to focus either on their personal needs or on those of their larger social network.

One way to serve a person's collectivist orientation is to show the benefits of your service to the individual as well as their larger social network. As an example, let's suppose I was trying to sell some advanced IT equipment to an IT executive from China. In doing so, I might stress how the new equipment would help the

[101] (Kamikaze, n.d.)
[102] (Goldberg, 2008)

company he works for as well as him. If I tried to sell the same type of equipment to an IT executive in the U.S., I might stress the benefits of the solution to help him do his job better, and then I'd follow that with company benefits.

Individualism and collectivism are two ends of a continuum. We are not either one or the other. But you may find that your customer leans more toward one orientation. Note the pronouns your customers use to determine where they fall on that continuum, and then use that information to serve them.

Monochronic and Polychronic Time Orientation

Yet another cultural difference relates to the perception or importance of time. The importance of time varies from culture to culture. For example, Western cultures tend to have a *monochronic* view of time, which means that keeping time and getting to places on time are critically important.

People with a monochronic view of time see time as linear, something that can be wasted, and even "killed[103]!"

In contrast, many other cultures have a *polychronic* sense of time. This means they tend to value the immediate experience or activity they're engaged in, and the people they're with rather than the time itself. As might be expected, people with a

103 (Gudykunst & Kim, 1997)

polychronic time orientation are not as concerned about being punctual as they are about the immediate situation in which they find themselves. Cultures that are polychronic can be found in South America, Africa, and the Middle East.

Imagine when someone with a polychronic time orientation meets up with someone who is monochronic. A polychronic person may show up late to a meeting. This will offend the monochronic, who rushes through the rest of the meeting, trying to get it back on track and stay on schedule. By so doing, the polychronic may view the monochronic as suspicious or arrogant or perhaps someone who is planning some insidious activity. So, before you jump down someone's throat because of a time issue, step back and make sure you understand the customer's culture.

Low-context and High-context Communication

Sometimes people say what they mean, while others don't mean what they say. Why? Because of their style of communication.

You'll find that people have two types of communication styles: low context and high context. People who use *low-context communication* say what they mean and mean what they say. That is, they rarely imply anything by what they say. Rather, they are literal, candid, and to the point. Western cultures tend to use low-context communication, as do men in general.

High-context communication is very different. In this communication style, people don't necessarily mean what they say. Rather, they tend to imply what they mean, often to avoid confrontation and to save face. A good example of high-context communication might go like this:

Two executives are working side by side late in the evening. One is especially tired but does not want to ask the other if they can call it a day. Rather than come out directly and state what she wants, she makes a comment like, "It's getting late. What time do we have to be back here tomorrow?" She didn't say she wanted to go to sleep. Instead, she implied it based on the context. By approaching things this way, she avoided being seen as the one who wanted to call it quits.

Most Eastern cultures and most women, use high-context communication styles. If you aren't paying attention to this style, you may think the person using it is just making conversation. Make sure you pay attention to the words and the context of communication because you'll often find there is more to it than what was said.

Power Distance

The way a culture values power and status are called *power distance*. Cultures can be either high-power distance or low-power distance.

A high-power-distance culture is one in which people of higher status see themselves as different from people of lower status and vice versa. Power is seen as a fact of life in big-power-distance cultures, where members stress coercive or referent power.

You will often find that a high-power-distance culture creates an authoritarian system where everybody knows their place. Countries like Saudi Arabia, India, Egypt, Guatemala, and Japan are high-power-distance.

Foreign students with a high-power-distance orientation are evident on U.S. university campuses. They will often regard the professor with great respect, showing deference through gestures, speech, and eye contact.

On the other hand, American students might address professors by their first name. That's because they have a low-power-distance orientation.

Low-power-distance cultures do not have as much regard for the power or status of a person. In a low-power-distance culture, it is quite common for a subordinate to question the orders of a superior when they want to understand why they are being asked to do something. Countries that are low-power-distance include the United States, Sweden, Germany, and Austria.

Imagine a subordinate from a low-power-distance culture who questions the orders of a superior from a high-power-distance culture. Can you guess the outcome? I would guess that they might be passed over for promotion, demoted, or even fired.

Now imagine a superior from a low-power-distance culture asking for the opinion of a subordinate from a high-power-distance culture. Do you think the subordinate will give his honest opinion? Certainly not.

You have to recognize the power-distance culture of your customer and learn how to use it effectively.

For example, if the person seems high-power-distance, show respect. If they seem low-power-distance, relax and engage them in friendly conversation.

Leverage intercultural insights to serve your customers the way they want to be served and you'll improve your service.

Chapter 16

The Duchenne Smile

We all have a need to be esteemed and treated with respect. This need is universal. If you serve this need in your customers, they will reward you with their love, loyalty, respect, and business.

The starting point for showing esteem is acknowledging the customer's presence. Nothing does this better than a smile and a warm greeting or good-bye. Smiling in particular seems to be an especially important tool in the development of personal and business relationships.

In terms of your personal relationships, many research studies demonstrate that when you smile you look more attractive to others[104]. That's because the geometry of your face changes to be more in accordance with the "golden ratio" or "divine proportions" of facial symmetry, which causes you to look more appealing[105].

In short, when you smile, you attract people.

---

[104] (Zebrowitz & Rhodes, 2002)

[105] (Marquardt Beauty Analysis, n.d.)

Research also shows that your smile will prompt others to smile. Smiling is contagious[106]. Remember the Law of Reciprocity? The person who initiates the smile can often influence the other person's reaction.

Smiling activates a specific muscle group called the zygomatic major muscle. This muscle group links to nerves that trigger a release of endorphins, which are natural opiates that relieve pain and make you feel good. Smiling also causes a release of serotonin into the bloodstream. This neurotransmitter acts as a mood enhancer, as well.

If you regularly smile at people and they smile back, you induce a chemical reaction in your brain and theirs. If you have recurring encounters with the same person and you smile at them and this person smiles back, you will eventually create a positive neurological association to you. They will want to be around you more and more.

If you supplement your smile with sincere compliments and words of encouragement, you will serve the emotional need for esteem and acceptance. When you serve a person's need for acceptance, you will cause that person to feel even better about you. They will start to think you are fantastic.

A smile can also influence a person's perceptions of your character traits. Generally speaking, a smile is likely to make people think you are generous, healthy, agreeable, and outgoing[107]. Depending on the social situation, these qualities may be brand-personality characteristics that you want others to perceive in you. Even if you don't think you have these traits, a good smile will convince others that you do.

Now that we know how smiling can alter your mood and make you feel better, perhaps it is no surprise that one way to treat

---

106 (Stibich, 2020)

107 (Selig, 2016)

depression, stress, and anxiety is to smile, because of the chemical reaction that occurs in your body. Researchers discovered that smiling creates a measurable reduction in your blood pressure, and it also boosts your immune system. Smiling has a tremendous impact on your well-being[108].

Try doing this yourself. Think of things that make you smile and then smile at other people. By taking control of how you feel and react to the world, you will be happier and healthier, and you will have many more friends.

The business benefits of smiling are also worth noting. Research has shown that employees who smile and exhibit warm and caring emotions impact the customer in the following ways:

- Influence purchase behavior
- Raise customer satisfaction
- Increase the amount of time spent in a store
- Cause customers to like the store
- Increase the customer's desire to return to the store
- Motivate customers to recommend the store[109]

Apparently, customers catch the emotional contagion of employees, and this feeling of well-being has a tremendous impact on customers.

In an informal research experiment, a professor at the University of California at San Diego tested the impact of a smile on the price of a product. To see if a smile affects the perceived value of a product, the professor divided his students into two groups and showed them faces of people. Group one viewed only pictures of neutral faces, while group two looked at neutral faces interspersed with smiling

---

108 (Zhivotovskaya, 2008)
109 (Abel & Abel, 2007)

faces. The professor then gave the student subjects some Kool Aid and asked them how much they would be willing to pay for it. Group two drank more Kool Aid and was willing to pay up to three times more than group one[110]. This means that when you smile at people you could influence their willingness to pay more and buy more.

Other experiments have shown that waitresses get larger tips if they give customers a big smile. A sincere smile will actually increase the customer's perception of your helpfulness and may help predispose the customer to a sales pitch[111].

Research on the impact of smiles on customer purchase behavior suggests big smiles increase customer perception of warmth with slight decreases in competence. When the consumption risk is low (buying a low-cost item) this works in favor of big smiles. When the consumption risk is high (buying a car, pitching for investment money to start a business) you may want to tone the smile down just a bit (Wang, MAO, LI, & LIU, 2017).

The Interaction Effect of Smile Intensity on Perceptions of Warmth and Competence

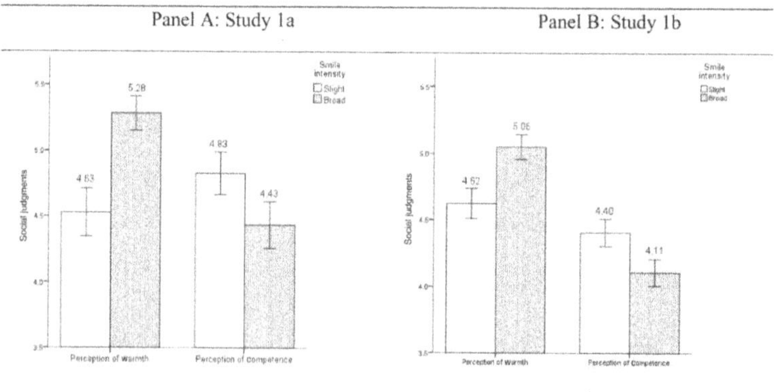

110 (htt10)

111 (Abel & Abel, 2007)

The Interaction Effect of Smile Intensity and Consumption Risk on Consumer Behavioral Intentions

Panel A: Behavioral intention

Panel B: Sign-up behavior

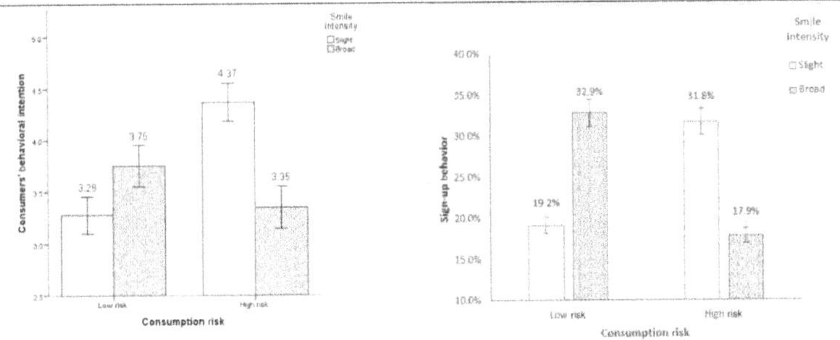

With all of these personal and business benefits of smiling, the only thing left to do is to make sure you know how to smile. The biggest smiles—the ones that are the sincerest—are the smiles you give to people you love or make when you're having a great time. Those are called "Duchenne smiles"[112].

A Duchenne smile is one where the corners of your mouth are turned up and the corner of the eyes are wrinkled like crow's feet[113]. That's your biggest smile, often associated with joy, happiness, excitement, or enthusiasm. This is the smile you want to use to get all those wonderful benefits we have discussed.

So, go ahead, smile!

112 (Zhivotovskaya , 2008)

113 (Duchenne smile, n.d.)

Chapter 17

Get in Rapport

The ability to develop rapport with people is perhaps the single most important soft skill you will ever learn. It will determine how successful you are in your personal relationships and in your business relationships. As an example, about eighty-three percent of all sales occur because the customer had a good rapport with the salesperson[114].

You have to develop a good rapport with your customers if you want to be successful. The *Merriam-Webster's Dictionary* defines *rapport* as a "relation marked by harmony, conformity, accord, or affinity[115]."

In essence, when you have a good rapport with someone, you like each other.

114 (Andreas, et al., 1994)

115 (Rapport, n.d.)

You can build rapport with customers in one of four ways. The four methods are nonverbal, verbal, tone, and touch. We will review each briefly.

Non-verbal

We need to do more than merely manage what we say. We also have to be careful about our non-verbal behavior. Consider the body language of your customers. Do they have to say they like you for you to determine if they do?

Usually not. You can often tell when someone likes you. How? To begin with, they show it.

When you like someone, you may unconsciously copy their behavior. We may mimic their posture, facial expressions, mannerisms, and even how they dress. We do this because we have a powerful need for love and belonging.

We tend to like people who act and speak the way we do and look and dress the way we do. One explanation for this phenomenon is that it reduces the physical and emotional distance between people. Research has shown that the physical proximity of people can influence liking. When those same people try to fit in and make connections with us, we can't help but increase our liking of them. Indeed, imitation is the sincerest form of flattery, but it is also the best way to build rapport with others.

Professional communicators know that an important strategy for building rapport with people is to imitate, match, or mirror them. Mirroring is a powerful technique that we all do unconsciously when we really like someone.

When you mirror someone, you match their tone of voice, emotional displays, body posture, facial expressions, rate of breathing, and gestures. This has to be done subtly; otherwise, the person will think you are mimicking them, and you will lose rapport. Rather, you need to adjust slowly. When you do, you will find that your rapport with that person will increase.

Next time you see two people interacting, notice whether or not they are mirroring each other and how their interaction is progressing as a result.

You will pick up a lot of information that will help you learn how to mirror people effectively to build rapport.

Another important way to achieve nonverbal rapport is to align your body physically with the customer's. *Alignment* means facing or sitting in the same direction as the customer rather than facing them directly. Research has shown that when you do this, you implicitly and explicitly communicate that you are with them instead of against them. This is an important way to let people know that you are "on their side." It also leads to a sense of togetherness and sharing if you decrease the space between the two of you, but make sure you maintain a reasonable distance, so you don't violate their physical space.

As you interact with your customer, you have to remember to maintain eye contact with them. Eye contact lets the other person know that you are interested in them. The "Like-Look Paradigm" says that we tend to look at what we like, and when we look longer, we are liked better[116]. How you look at customers will affect their perception of you, so be kind.

---

[116] (Goleman, 2006, 2007)

Verbal

Developing verbal rapport with customers is important as well. There are two ways to do this. The first is related to *word choice*[117]. Research has shown that those who use negative words, especially obscene words, cause others to form negative judgments. In contrast, people who use positive words were found to be more socially attractive. Additionally, moderate use of intense words to convey action and enthusiasm can have a positive social effect. *Amazing*, *spectacular*, *fantastic*, and *brilliant* are all good examples.

The second way you can create verbal rapport is by talking about subjects the customer finds interesting. People enjoy talking about their interests. If you have done your research and have discovered your customer's interests, try asking about them and see what happens. You'll find they will light up. That positive emotion and your sincere interest will strengthen your interpersonal relationship. The feelings you elicit will be associated with you.

Tone

[117] (Goleman, 2006, 2007)

As you adjust your nonverbal and verbal behavior, you should also match the tone and rhythm of your speech with your customer's. Doing this can either help create rapport or destroy it.

A major regional telephone company used tone and rhythm matching to improve customer service interactions, taking it from the lowest in satisfaction ratings to one of the top three spots[118]. When you are able to achieve dramatic improvements such as these, the technique speaks for itself.

Touch

The last part of building rapport is *touchy*. I'm being literal and corny at the same time. But seriously, touch has the potential to be a very powerful force in affecting people.

Generally speaking, a touch on the hand, arm, or shoulder during the course of a conversation can have moderate to very pleasant effects on the customer. Even if the "customer" is a stranger, a touch on the arm can have a positive effect, according to research studies on interpersonal relationships.

The intention of your touch should be only a part of a natural conversation, greeting, or goodbye. If you touch somebody without

---

[118] (Andreas, et al., 1994)

such a context, you will likely have some problems, so please use caution.

We have reviewed a lot of the mechanical aspects of creating rapport. These techniques, however, lack an emotional component, which is necessary for you to truly be in tune with others, so don't make a ritual of them.

Research suggests that your emotional state and your expressions should reflect those of your customer. By doing this, you are letting them know that you are acknowledging their feelings. If your customer is upset, let yourself feel and show that. Agree with the customer. When you do this, they will relax a bit. Then, you should ask them to explain the problem so that you can understand it.

Finally, the best communicators actually do the least communicating. They listen instead. Customers like listeners because they allow them to talk. Listening leads others to believe that you care about their needs and situation.

You can increase your level of rapport with others simply by listening attentively, mirroring behavior, offering affirmations, asking questions in order to gain clarity, and paraphrasing what you heard.

Sometimes you don't need to provide a solution. You just need to listen, and then people will feel better. People who listen more than they talk are liked better, and customers rate them as more competent compared to those who do more talking[119]. Truly listening to customers is one of the most important ways to identify breakthrough product ideas.

Are you listening?

---

119 (Goleman, 2006, 2007)

CHAPTER 18

You Must Be the Feel-Good Doctor

According to some well-regarded research, you'll find six reasons why you might lose customers[120].

1. Customers leave because they died (one percent).
2. Customers leave because they moved away (three percent).
3. Customers leave because a friend recommended another solution (five percent).
4. Customers leave for a better product or service (nine percent).
5. Customers are lost because of dissatisfaction (fourteen percent).
6. Customers leave because they feel unappreciated, unimportant, and taken for granted (sixty-eight percent).

---

[120] (Maguire, 2007)

I find it amazing that sixty-eight percent leave because they don't feel appreciated. My guess is that just about every kind of customer relationship (paying, personal, employee, or other) is lost for the same reasons with about the same percentage distribution.

Even in the most sacred of all relationships, marriage, people seem to forget the importance of expressing their appreciation. In a study that involved 168 couples over thirteen years, researchers found that the lack of love and affection in marriage is the single greatest cause of divorce. No, it's not about financial issues[121].

Expressing appreciation is also important in the workplace. A U.S. Department of Labor report found because the number-one reason employees leave is that they don't feel appreciated[122].

You don't want to lose your customers, so you have to make sure they feel appreciated. Let's look at some things we can do to generate positive feelings with customers, so they don't leave us.

Giving sincere and honest compliments is one of the best ways to create a positive feeling in others. Your compliments can be either focused on attributes specific to a person or things that a person has accomplished. Either one will be well received but, depending on the relationship you have with your customer, one may be more appropriate than the other. For instance, in a professional situation you should focus on complimenting behaviors, although giving personal compliments in a professional setting can work just as well. They often have positive and lasting psychological benefits that can alter performance.

In the late 1960s a teacher from Riceville, Iowa, was deeply moved by the assassination of Dr. Martin Luther King. She then decided to devise a cultural exercise to teach her all-white, third-grade class the inherent evils of racism. The exercise required

[121] (Interesting Divorce Statistics, Facts, and Rate, n.d.)
[122] (Rath & Clifton, 204)

the children to be segregated into two groups according to eye color. The blue-eyed group was given special privileges, told that they were superior in intelligence, and allowed to demoralize the brown-eyed group. The brown-eyed children were made to wear ribbons around their neck to symbolize their inferiority. They were denied basic rights, told that they were inferior, and were made to endure abusive behavior. This went on for one day, and then the roles were reversed the next day so that the brown-eyed children were the superior group. The exercise generated a lot of controversy locally, nationally, and then globally.

Overlooked was the effect of the experiment. The children in the superior group acted arrogant and bossy, but their grades improved, and they performed math and reading tasks beyond their previous skill level[123]. Meanwhile, the children in the inferior group became timid and subservient, and their academic performance suffered.

In fact, the children in the inferior group had trouble completing tasks that had previously been simple for them. This exercise was repeated hundreds of times by the teacher, and the results were the same.

This exercise proves the tremendous power that compliments and criticism, can have on the thoughts and ability of our customers. You can improve the performance of your customers if you find ways to compliment them. Likewise, you can improve the performance of your children, your spouse, your friends, your coworkers, or anyone else. People will believe the good things you tell them, and that belief will promote their psychological well-being.

Laughter is another powerful way to generate positive feelings in your customers. Laughing lowers the level of stress hormones,

[123] (Jane Elliott, n.d.)

boosts the immune system, and improves the function of blood vessels. That's why you feel so relaxed after a good laugh. Research shows that laughter might even prevent heart disease[124]. It can also reduce your blood sugar levels and increase glucose tolerance in diabetics and non-diabetic people[125].

Emotionally, laughter releases endorphins into the bloodstream, which as we discussed before, is a naturally occurring opiate that makes people feel good and reduces pain[126]. When you are able to make people laugh, you are able to control a chemical reaction that causes them to feel better. If you can help make people laugh consistently, they can't help but like you. You will become addictive. They will want to have you around, even though they can't explain why.

Making people laugh also has significant social benefits. First of all, laughter is contagious. When you laugh at something, others will laugh, too, which will create the health and emotional benefits just described. Laughter also makes us socially attractive. People want to be around others who laugh because that makes them laugh. Not surprisingly, people often cite a good sense of humor as an important trait they look for in a spouse. They want their mate to make them feel good.

Laughter benefits you too, when you make others laugh. First, you get all the health, emotional, and social rewards just described. Second, laughing helps you dissociate yourself from a bad situation, making it easier for you to cope with problems or problematic people. Your life will change for the better when you laugh. Just don't laugh too loud or too long. That could scare everybody!

---

[124] (Laughter is the "Best Medicine" for Your Heart, n.d.)

[125] (Laughter: The Best Medicine, n.d.)

[126] (Laughter is the Best Medicine, n.d.)

I'm not suggesting that you be a clown and do anything and everything to make people laugh. I'm just asking you to serve your life customers by getting them to laugh regularly. The benefits of doing so are quite clear.

You can get your life customers to laugh by taking them to comedy shows or funny movies. You can tell jokes, make puns, and point out the funny things in life. But don't be vulgar or make fun of other people or put them down. Don't be cynical or self-deprecating. By doing so, you will hurt only yourself and others. In fact, having a cynical outlook on life can have dangerous consequences for your heart health, according to a research study of 6,814 people[127]. Always maintain a positive outlook.

You might wonder about the business benefits to all of this laughing. In fact, the business benefits can be profound. First, laughing helps lower stress levels and improves health generally, which could lower the health care costs of your employees.

Second, laughter improves group cooperation and productivity. In addition, customer satisfaction will improve, relationships will lengthen, and profits will expand by focusing on building a positive relationship based in part on laughter. And that's no joke.

The last key strategy for delivering superior customer service is offering a little surprise now and then. Find ways to show random acts of kindness or little unexpected ways to make people feel good.

Have you ever been surprised by someone's kindness? Then you know how this feels. People can't help but feel special and appreciated when you surprise them with kind acts. This is true in both personal and professional settings.

In fact, one of the best ways to show appreciation to your customer and employees is by doing so outside a formal rewards program.

---

[127] (Cynicism link with heart disease, 2007)

Formal rewards programs become an entitlement, whereas unplanned rewards are not. Research shows that employees prefer unplanned rewards and praise for a job well done versus planned rewards and praise[128]. When you praise employees, their brain releases dopamine into their blood[129]. That makes them feel good.

Anyone receiving praise feels the same way. So, don't be stingy with your praise. Find ways to shower it on people when they least expect it, and it will have a profound impact on them and your relationship with them.

When it comes to paying customers, many companies try to create customer loyalty by using formal rewards programs that offer them "points" or other forms of compensation. These rewards programs do not build true loyalty. They *buy* loyalty. Such systems are a form of operant conditioning.

Operant conditioning intends to reward, or punish, in response to a behavior. If you do something good, you get a reward. However, when a reward is expected it becomes an entitlement.

Instead of setting up an entitlement system for customer reward programs, surprise them with rewards. The effect of an unexpected reward will heighten emotional response, building relationship affinity that is far more powerful than a bunch of reward points or discounts.

---

128 http://info.4imprint.com/wp-content/uploads/Employee%20Recognition_final.pdf

129 (Barrett, 2009)

Chapter 19

Handling Irate People

"Today is a good day," Martha tells herself as she gets ready for work, but deep down, Martha is a sad person. She has had to endure many bad experiences for as long as she can remember. Nothing ever seems to go her way.

Martha grew up in a broken home and was often abused by her stepfather. The physical and mental abuse caused her to feel alone, insecure, and ashamed, so much so that when she got to high school, she instantly fell in love with her first boyfriend. Soon thereafter, she became pregnant and dropped out of school to give birth to and take care of her little boy.

Things were hard at first because her boyfriend left her as soon as he found out she was pregnant. She had to do everything on her own and depended on public assistance to get by. She moved often from place to place, usually crammed into whatever spare room she could find among friends and distant relatives.

As her son grew, Martha became motivated to do the very best she could for him, so she decided to get a job and enroll in community college. She was determined to build a better life for her son and herself.

Things seemed to be turning around for Martha when she got a job as a cashier at a national discount retailer. She was so excited. The job even included health benefits after six months of work. Now she was able to take evening classes at a local community college, where she studied to get her associates degree in nursing. Her days were exhausting, but visions of her son kept her going.

Two weeks ago, she learned that her son had a debilitating bone disease that would require weekly hospital visits and painful treatment. Ever since she learned the bad news, Martha has been feeling emotionally drained and heartbroken. Fortunately, her health insurance at work will cover all the costs, but she has been in a panic lately because the store manager keeps talking about cutting back everyone's hours and laying off as many as ten people. She worries about losing her job, which would force her and her son out on the street.

Martha never complains much, so you'd never know she had all these challenges. In fact, everyone thinks of her as very quiet and shy. She smiles all the time, but her face shows the worry and fear that plague her. The sagging skin under her eyes indicates someone who has walked a path of sorrows for a long time.

When Martha walks into the store where she works, she hears the bustle of commerce at the checkout stands that mark her station in life. She automatically smiles at several associates she knows well and heads to the employee break room, where she puts her things away and prepares for a full day of work. Just then the hardships of her life really hit her, and she flees to the lady's room to weep silently in a bathroom stall. After a few minutes, she composes herself, washes her face, puts on her smock, and proceeds to the front of the store. There she opens her register and turns on the light above her checkout stand to indicate that she is open for business, but in truth she feels closed off and alone in her life.

Martha softly calls out to the people lined up in the checkout lane beside hers, "I can help you over here." A young woman at the back of the line hurries to Martha's station and quickly unloads a mountain of items from her cart. The woman is well dressed but disheveled and obviously worn out by her whining little girl. The woman pays for her things, gives Martha a contrived smile, and then pushes her heavy cart toward the exit.

Martha's next customer is extremely angry because he was next in line in the checkout lane beside Martha's when she called out for the next customer. The young woman with the overloaded cart had beaten him to Martha's lane, and he had to wait a good five minutes before he got his turn. When he did, he was locked, loaded, and ready to fire at someone.

Gary is having a bad day. He has just learned that he might not get a major sales account that he has been working on for more than eight months.

He is agitated because he spent so much time on a deal that might fall through.

When Gary gets to Martha, he tells her that she is the most incompetent person that he has ever met.

"You're too damn slow," he says. "You should've called me over to the line first, you idiot. They made a big mistake when they hired you." He continued to take out his frustration on Martha the whole time she waited on him.

Tears streamed down Martha's face as she handed Gary his receipt and said, "Have a nice day." Gary told her where to stick her nice day, then headed to the customer service counter to complain about her.

Martha's heart pounded as she sobbed. Would this be it? Would she lose her job? Images of she and her son living on the street flashed in her mind.

Gary is an *irate customer* who verbally and emotionally assaulted Martha. His actions are neither appropriate nor justified. Even though he didn't break any law, he broke the rules of common decency. He did so because he knew that he occupied the more powerful position and that he wouldn't suffer any personal, social, or professional consequence for his behavior. In essence, he knew he could verbally abuse Martha as a way to take out his frustrations with impunity, so that is what he did.

People like Gary are usually plagued by a number of personal problems that rarely have anything to do with the situation at hand. Their behavior demonstrates a poor ability to deal with the problems they have. To cope, they take out their anger on others. This is called displaced aggression.

Displaced aggression occurs when we unjustly take out our frustrations or anger on something or someone[130]. In such an instance, we beat up people who aren't the cause of our feelings. This isn't fair, but it happens.

Have you ever had a customer service person treat you rudely? Most of us have. I find it interesting how those experiences make me feel. I used to get angry with rude people. I'd even go so far as to be rude back. That was a mistake.

"Every obnoxious act is a cry for help," said the famous sales consultant Zig Ziglar. Rude people aren't bad people. They just

---

[130] (Displaced Aggression, n.d.)

don't feel well. Maybe someone was rude to them, or maybe they've had a very bad day or an unhappy life.

They are reflecting onto you the painful emotions they're feeling because of the way other people have treated them. In psychoanalysis, this is known as transference.

The sooner you realize this, the better off you will be. Yet, most people get drawn into the venomous attacks of an irate customer because they are almost always personal. Don't fall into that trap, or else you'll get hurt.

Do Not Fight Back

When an irate customer attacks you, do not fight back or become defensive. Justified or not, making a counterattack will immediately create a bad brand association. That will only escalate the tension between you and the customer.

Instead of fighting back, mentally reject the abuse. Do not reject it verbally. A verbal response is fighting back. Just tell yourself that you don't accept the abuse. Keep your cool. Try to help the customer. If that doesn't work, find someone to help you.

Dissociate Yourself from the Abuse

When we are engaged with someone, we associate into the experience. A good example is laughing with friends about something funny. In a situation like this, we often forget ourselves and get caught up in the moment.

The same thing happens when we become angry with someone who has made a personal attack on us.

We completely associate into the moment. We fight to defend ourselves. We've all had the experience of being cut off by a discourteous driver, thus "road rage." We associate into what's happening in that moment and take it personally. Certain fingers are often used to express how we feel. Personally, I'm a big fan of the thumbs-up gesture, but to each his own.

Your angry response to negative stimulation illustrates how an irate customer can have a tremendous influence on how you feel. If you let them, your customers can control you. They can make you smile, or they can make you cry if you let them, meaning that you are giving them the choice of which kind of product they want you to be. That is a very disempowering way for you to live. We need to control our feelings by deciding what we want to associate into and dissociate from. When we dissociate from something, we mentally distance ourselves from the situation.

When you dissociate from a situation, in your mind's eye, you may be able to observe your body and others around it as separate from your mental self, as if you were having an out-of-body-experience. While this might sound a little too New Age for you, this is something we do all the time. In fact, you dissociate from things more often than you think.

If you have ever been around someone you think is not at your level, or if you have ever been in a place that did not meet your standards, you likely dissociated yourself. You may have thought this person or place wasn't acceptable, so you mentally distanced yourself. The ability to dissociate or associate is a very powerful technique to use for managing your state of mind[131].

Dealing with irate customers is usually an emotional interaction, and therefore it is easy to associate into it. For you to remain in control of yourself as the product, try to dissociate from it while trying to understand the customer and what they need. Asking yourself questions about why the customer is acting the way they are can help you separate yourself from the emotion of the situation.

Try to Understand

If you have an irate customer, you need to understand that they became that way because of some bad experience they had. That experience may or may not involve you directly, but it doesn't matter whether it did or not. Try to understand the customer's grievance.

---

131 (Andreas, et al., 1994)

Allowing people to blow off steam will help you to understand their complaint and find a solution. Sometimes, though, we may feel defensive because the irate customer complains about something we did or someone or something we care about. Such a response will do nothing to improve the situation. Rather, it will only entrench you in opposition.

Allow the customer to make accusations and claims. Without argument, observe carefully and try to determine if the grievance is sufficient to justify the outburst. If it is not, the customer may have been upset by something else.

Show Your Empathy

People may tell you to remain calm when dealing with an irate customer, but this strategy has the exact opposite effect of the one you want. Upset customers don't calm down when you are calm. They often get angrier because they view your calm behavior as indifference.

If the customer is mad about something that would make you mad, too, then allow yourself to be upset along with them. Doing this establishes rapport and validates the customer's feelings, which will calm them down[132]. You are also showing the customer that their dissatisfaction has a valid basis and that you agree with them.

---

132 (Andreas, et al., 1994)

This is the same response you'd have if your friend told you about an unpleasant experience. Why not think of your customers as friends? If you do, they will see you as an advocate, not an enemy. Remember that empathy is not an admission of guilt. Just because you allow yourself to express your agreement with the customer does not mean you agree with their claim. You are simply validating their emotions. You need to accept their feelings and then focus on becoming their advocate while you try to gather all the facts and determine the validity of their claim. The *customer is always right until proven otherwise.*

Quickly Admit Fault if You Find Fault

Early in 2010, the world watched the Toyota Motor Corporation deal with claims that some of their cars had accelerated spontaneously, which in some cases had caused the death of their customers. During its initial public defense, Toyota claimed that the problem was caused by defective floor mats.

Industry experts questioned that explanation. They knew that Toyotas had an electronic acceleration and braking system, which could have malfunctioned for any number of reasons. Such a defect would likely cost Toyota much more to correct than replacing faulty floor mats. *The Wall Street Journal* reported that Toyota officials considered it a "win" when they were able to lobby federal safety officials and limit the recall cost to $100 million[133].

While the true nature of the acceleration problem will take some time to identify, the president of Toyota blamed his company's quality problems on "excessive focus on market share and profits[134]." Other top executives said that they had lost their focus on the customer. Those are brave things to say—and the right thing to admit.

What a fall from grace, though. The once mighty Toyota had been synonymous with good customer service and top-quality products. But somehow it had lost that focus and became so engrossed with profit and growth that it was willing to down play quality problems. That cost them dearly. During the first part of 2010, Toyota's profits plummeted as it dealt with massive recalls, declining sales, and bad public relations.

In business and in your personal life, you must quickly admit your mistakes and take immediate action to correct them.

By doing so, you will give yourself a chance to right your wrongs and keep your customer from going to the competition.

Overcompensate for Your Error

133 (King & Mitchell, 2010)

134 (Shirouzu,, 2010)

A textbook case for the best public relations response by a company in the face of a terrible public scare happened in the U.S. during the 1980s, when the makers of Tylenol pulled their product off the shelf when cases of tampering were identified. The company came out early to address the issue and devised a way to make their products tamper-proof. Their focus was on the well-being of their customers. They generated a lot of favorable publicity, increased customer loyalty, and boosted profits.

Tylenol's manufacturers probably didn't have to take such drastic action, but by doing so, they sent a powerful message to their customers: they cared more about their long-term relationship with them than a short-term profit. They overcompensated for a situation that was not directly their fault. By doing something extraordinary to protect their customers, they received something extraordinary in return.

If you have an irate customer, overcompensate them if they have a legitimate grievance against you or your company. Your willingness to accept responsibility for your faults and make restitution will help improve your standing.

Forgive Quickly

Your irate customers may be wrong to treat you the way they do. Even though they give you reasons that support their behavior, those reasons probably won't justify their bad behavior. If you have been maligned, your tendency will be to resent your customers, but you must let go of that resentment.

An act of forgiveness is done more for you than for the other person. When you forgive someone, you improve interpersonal relationships. Consider that most conflict is a misunderstanding—and failure to communicate properly. When you realize this, you can let things roll off your back and remain in a positive state of mind.

Some irate customers will try to hijack your good mood and replace it with a bad one, but if you forgive them quickly, you will be able to maintain a positive disposition no matter what they do.

If you learn to forgive others, it will reduce stress, lower your blood pressure, minimize depression, and reduce the risk of substance abuse. In fact, forgiveness is often an important part of dealing with substance abuse and addictions. You will find that by forgiving someone you will engender a tremendous healing in yourself and in your relationships.

Take a Lunch Break

Sometimes the best way to handle an irate customer is to take a break from them. This should be a time to check in with yourself and reflect on how you're feeling. It's also a good opportunity for you to decompress and get your mind off this person. They shouldn't own your thoughts. So, take a break once in a while.

Chapter 20

The Rocking Chair Test

It's about 9pm on a Thursday night and I've just sat down to write. I am trying to recess into that state of flow when I hear tap, tap, tap. It's the door to my home office. *Tap, tap, tap.* There it is again.

I get up from my chair and approach the door to open it when I hear scratching against the door. I open the door and look down to see my 17-month-old daughter who then says, "Hi!"

Without any hesitation she proceeds to march into my office and heads straight for my chair.

I tell her, "No, no, honey. Daddy is working right now. You have to go with Mommy."

I take her by the hand and lead her out the door. I go to sit back in my chair. I'm now trying to get back to that state of flow. Deep thought takes over.

Tap, tap, tap. "Is that the baby again," I think to myself? Somewhat frustrated, I go to the door, open it up and look down to see my daughter with her beautiful little arm extended up toward me with a little pop-up toy in hand.

"No thank you, honey. I don't want that. Why don't you give that to mommy," I said. I again scoot her away.

I go to sit down in my chair and I turn around to face my bookcase. I am trying to change my perspective so I might find inspiration to begin writing. That's when I notice that my door is cracked open. I forgot to close it all the way.

Just about the time I realize this, the baby pushes the door open again, same toy in hand, and says, "Hi!" She runs over to the side of my chair, puts her little head on my leg, and says, "Aaahh," which is something we all utter around the house when we see her do something caring, loving, or sweet to someone else.

I realize now that she wants my love. She wants my attention. She wants me to play with her. But I'm busy so I scoot her away once more and go back to my chair.

I feel bad by now and my mind suddenly takes me on a journey. I imagine it is 20 years into the future and I'm in my office. I am observing myself typing on the computer when suddenly I'm taken to outside of the door of my office to watch my little girl all grown up, cautiously approaching the door with her hands clasped together. She raises her hand to knock but pulls it back and instead moves her head close to the door as if to listen to what the older me is doing in the office. She pulls her head away, turns around, and walks away.

She learned to stop knocking.

I'm moved and emotional. I don't want to be that person. Rushing out of my chair, I open the door to find my little girl at the door again. I pick her up and hold her in my arms while I stare into her eyes. I realize that she is only going to be this little for a while and then this time will be gone and I will have lost this precious moment to play with her and show her that I love her. If I don't stop and build that relationship with her now, if I don't make time for her now, she might stop knocking. If she stops knocking I will lose that opportunity to make that connection with her and be part of this wonderful being that has come into my life.

That's when it hit me. We have to be available to our customers, all of them, when they come knocking.

Are you opening the door when opportunity knocks?

Tap tap tap. It's me. I'm knocking on the door to your life. I'm asking you to let me in for a minute so I can share something with you. Please don't turn me away. I want to help you. I want to share what I have learned with you.

Will you open up the door? Will you let me in to help you? I hope so, but I can only hope. It's up to you to open the door.

The Rocking Chair Test

Have you ever heard of the rocking chair test? If not, let me explain it to you.

The rocking chair test asks you to imagine how you feel at the end of your life based on how you are living today. If you feel great, then you passed the test and you are well on your way to the life you want. If you feel regret, you failed the test and you need to make immediate change now.

I want you to take the rocking chair test.

Imagine you are 20, 30 or even 40 years older than you are now. You are at the end of your life. You are coming out of the front door of a home you live in with eyes pointed toward an old wooden rocking chair. You head for the chair as the screen door whacks back to slap shut. You slowly but assuredly make your way to the chair, you sit down, and begin to rock. Imagine it in your mind.

Now I want you to think about yourself in that chair and imagine back to this time when you read this book, even this very instance. I want you to imagine that you decided you didn't need to treat everyone like a customer. Imagine you kept on living the way you've always done before because you decided you didn't need to change.

As you imagine yourself sitting in the rocking chair, many years into the future, think how your life turned out. Did you become a super success like you always hoped you would become or was life a disappointment? Did you open life's doors when you heard *tap, tap, tap* or did you keep them shut? Are you happy with the way things turned out or do you feel regret?

Think about it.

If you found your life isn't what you hoped it would be, I want you to do something for yourself. Resolve to change. Resolve to open the door to your customers, all of them, when you hear tap, tap, tap.

Do things with a smile. Treat everyone like a customer. You will find, just like I did on a dark Thursday evening in December, that where you least expect to find success and inspiration, it is there you will find it.

That's the Hidden Fortune of Service.

Chapter 21

Re-write Your Fortune

Our success is measured by our service to others and our failure is quantified by our lack thereof. We profit when customers give us something of value that is greater than what we gave them. We lose when we fail to honestly serve the needs of others.

Profiting from customers requires us to deliver exceptional value. That doesn't mean the value we deliver has to be less than the cost of it. Value is defined in the eyes of the beholder.

Did you know that the American Indians sold the island of Manhattan to Dutch traders for approximately $24 worth of beads? At least that's what the American history books say. This may not be entirely accurate, however.

In 1626, Dutch colonist Peter Schagen wrote a letter to the directors of the West India Company. He told them about the purchase of the island of Manhattan. In that letter he said: "We have bought the island of Manhattes from the savages for a value of 60 guilders." That translates into about $24. He made no mention of beads.

American Indians were notoriously savvy traders. They reportedly took payment in the form of "fabric, axes, hoes, awls, kettles, Jews' harps, as well as beads[135]." So, historians believe that the trade was made for more than just beads. The same Europeans also purchased Staten Island for 60 guilders worth of such goods[136].

Considering the manufacturing capabilities of American Indians in 1626, these items would have represented an enormous value. Furthermore, cultural anthropologists believe that the Native Americans didn't think they were selling land, because the very idea that it could be sold was as preposterous to them as selling air. The cultural anthropologists think the Indians were merely accepting a peace offering for sharing the land without bloodshed. They probably thought they were renting out the joint for a lot of value.

Value is in the eyes of the beholder. If you deliver value to customers at a lower cost than what it takes to make a product, you will profit.

If you don't, you won't.

In most cases, we lose in life because we are so focused on ourselves that we fail to serve the needs of others. We get so caught up in serving our own interests that we are willing to do anything to get what we want. We then become prey to the doctrine of a false profit and its seductive get-rich-quick schemes. This sophistry often leads to a terrible loss.

In January 2010, British Sky Broadcasting Group (BskyB) won a £700 million legal battle against EDS, a division of Hewlett Packard. Why? Because BskyB claimed that an EDS salesperson had misrepresented the timeline and ultimate cost of the *system it purchase*d, and the British courts agreed[137]. This is one of the

---

[135] (Soniak, 2012)
[136] (Marton, 2015)
[137] (Sonne, 2010)

largest judgments in history against an IT services provider, and it will almost assuredly cause a change in how business is done in the UK.

In February 2010, EDS made what the British courts called an interim payment of £200 million, but the cost to the company was far greater[138]. First, the legal costs alone have been described as the largest in history for such a case—about £40 million[139]. The negative press coverage most likely cost EDS future sales because potential customers got scared off and existing customers defected. The resulting impact on the company's brand will no doubt cause some future prospects to turn to other more credible providers, forcing EDS to compete even harder on price. Such action will lower profitability.

If we try to maximize short-term economic gain, we may be persuaded to focus on serving customers by overpromising and underdelivering or to say and do something unethical. The economics of doing this ensures a long-term challenge for building wealth.

If you want to succeed, you must provide the greatest value at the lowest cost to the most people. If you can do that, you'll ride a wave of success. Serve everyone like a customer, and you'll be able to identify the best opportunities for riding that wave.

Blake Mycoskie stumbled upon a novel way to provide value to lots of people while he was competing in the popular American TV show, *The Amazing Race*. During the competition, when Mycoskie was in Argentina, he noticed that many of the children didn't have shoes because they were too poor to afford them. When he returned to Argentina in 2006 for a vacation, he decided to start

---

[138] (HP must pay $315 million to BSkyB, 2010)

[139] (htt11)

a shoe company that would solve this problem. Thus, the TOMS shoe company was born.

For TOMS flagship offering, Mycoskie decided to adapt a native Argentine shoe called the *alpargata* to sell in the American market. He then created the One for One™ promise to American consumers who bought his shoes. The program worked like this: For every pair of shoes Americans bought, TOMS promised to donate one pair of shoes to children in need. The shoes and the promise became a hit almost immediately. In the first four years, TOMS generated an estimated $50 million in sales and provided over one million shoes to children worldwide.

TOMS serve customers' need to give and their need for shoes. As a result, the concept has spawned a new business model—the social enterprise. People can now buy things that serve their immediate needs as well as the needs of others. This taps into a latent human desire to give. For those who buy them, TOMS shoes have become a badge of social consciousness and a fashionable style all in one.

TOMS shoes aren't expensive to make, but they are expensive to buy. The average price is somewhere between $50 and $60, So, why do people buy what amounts to a canvassed slipper? The shoes sell because TOMS give people a way to serve a need to give back. This taps into a latent human need for many (e.g. Intellectual Needs).

By setting out to serve the needs of disadvantaged children and the needs of others who want to help them, TOMS has profited from its relationships in new and inspiring ways. TOMS was created to serve everyone like a customer, and in the process, Mycoskie created became wealthy and made the world a better place to live. You, too, can discover such opportunities when you are focused on serving the needs of others.

Remember, every person has value to you and every person is valuable. Even the homeless man you pass by on the street has value to you and is valuable. You might think that's impossible. You might be surprised just as one woman was during a cold New York night.

April 26, 2010 the New York Post reported that a homeless man was killed after coming to the rescue of a complete stranger. The good Samaritan thrust himself between a woman and a man armed with a knife, and he was stabbed several times in the process. This hero then wandered the streets of Queens, New York searching for help but he wouldn't find it.

Surveillance cameras captured the homeless man, Hugo Alfredo Tale-Yax, dying in a pool of blood on a street. The cameras record a man bending down to turn over Hugo's lifeless body but then he walks away. He does nothing to help. Two more men stop to have a conversation about Hugo and one takes a picture. They do nothing to help.

Twenty-five people would walk past Hugo without ever trying to help him. They are indifferent to the world. They are mired in a situational-value system, and as a result they are tuned out to the needs of others they see as worthless. Yet, Hugo would give his life trying to help these very same people.

It has been said there is no greater love than someone who lays down his life for his friends. I wonder how much more love a person must have if they lay down their life for a stranger. Perhaps, just perhaps, this is the greatest act of service a person can give.

Many men and women of your country's armed services made such a sacrifice, and with great honor. Yet, Hugo wore no uniform. He took no pledge. He held no station of esteem.

Perhaps you might think that Hugo's act of service gave him nothing in return. A homeless man would leave this Earth alone, cold and dying on a city street, after making the ultimate sacrifice. But, as Fortune would have it, that man was made a hero by a surveillance camera. He is now memorialized as an example of the best of all mankind. He demonstrated the highest values we strive to practice. He, who many would say was the least among us, was made the greatest among us. How ironic.

The Hidden Fortune of Service is a powerful force. You can't stop it from chasing you down and repaying you. Every act of serviceis rewarded—either by the recipient or by some other means. Even now, in this book, Hugo's service is being honored and it will be again and again forever more.

You can re-write your fortune in life, no matter your life stage or situation. It's never too late. If you take the first step and serve everyone like a customer, you will unlock a wealth of opportunity in every area of your life and you'll build a better society in the process.

The greatest among us serve all of us.

That's the Hidden Fortune of Service.

About the Author

"Great perspective and advice to personally and professionally succeed in any economic situation."

– Dak Liyanearachchi, Chief Analytical Officer, NRG Energy, Inc.

Kris Chettayar has worked as an executive and consultant for some of the largest Fortune 1000 companies in the world. His work has helped companies generate billions of dollars in revenue annually. Chettayar completed a master's in management and engineering and a master's degree in marketing and data science from Northwestern University. He graduated from California State University, Fullerton, with a Bachelor of Arts in marketing. Chettayar can be reached at www.chettayar.com.

A Way Out: The Hidden Fortune of Service

Personal setbacks. Professional challenges. Company obstacles. National dilemmas. They happen to everyone and have occurred in every generation throughout time. Sometimes they are the result of our choices, but a great many times, our situation is the result of things outside of our control. The year 2020 is a good example.

A Way Out: The Hidden Fortune of Service, written by an executive and consultant to Fortune 1000 companies, details the mindset and practices of the richest individuals, businesses, and nations in the world. It takes the reader on a journey into the central driver of wealth and provides the science and techniques to harness it for personal and professional success in any circumstance. The book gives an inside view of ordinary people who have lifted themselves out of challenging circumstances to achieve extraordinary things.

This is a must-read for people who are looking to find a way to survive and thrive in any economic situation because it isn't over until it's over. There is still time to re-write your fortune. *There is A Way Out!*

Bibliography

(n.d.). Retrieved from theodora.com: http://www.theodora.com/wfb1989/soviet_union/soviet_union_economy.html

(n.d.). Retrieved from reuters.com: https://www.reuters.com/article/pressRelease/idUS176233+04-Jun-2008+PRN20080604

(n.d.). Retrieved from pacificsource.com: http://www.pacificsource.com/PDFs/article_workstress_06.pdf

(n.d.). Retrieved from mindpub.com: http://www.mindpub.com/art472.htm

(n.d.). Retrieved from healthywomen.com: http://www.healthywomen.org/presskit/stress/pg5.html

(n.d.). Retrieved from gurusoftware.com: http://www.gurusoftware.com/GuruNet/Personal/Topics/Values.htm

(n.d.). Retrieved from findcounseling.com: http://www.findcounseling.com/help/news/2006/09/teens_underuse_empathy_region.html

(n.d.). Retrieved from chrisgardnermedia.com: https://www.chrisgardnermedia.com

(n.d.). Retrieved from cancer.gov: https://www.cancer.gov/Templates/db_alpha.aspx?CdrID=44928

(n.d.). Retrieved from Business Week: http://images.businessweek.com/ss/10/02/0218_customer_service_champs/index.htm

(n.d.). Retrieved from Business Week: http://retailindustry.about.com/gi/o.htm?zi=1/XJ&zTi=1&sdn=retailindustry&cdn=money&tm=102&gps=359_726_1259_548&f=10&su=p554.13.336.ip_&tt=2&bt=0&bts=0&zu=http%3A//www.businessweek.com/magazine/content/09_09/b4121030589997.htm

(n.d.). Retrieved from http://www.itworld.com/legal/94442/bskyb-wins-709m-lawsuit-against-hp-eds

(n.d.). Retrieved from http://dsc.discovery.com/news/2008/01/03/smile-communication-02.html

(n.d.). Retrieved from http://www.google.com/imgres?q=cingulate+cortex&start=210&num=10&um=1&hl=en&biw=1366&bih=601&tbm=isch&tbnid=QSOPrU45ccvwfM:&imgrefurl=http://www.dana.org/news/brainhealth/detail.aspx%3Fid%3D10010&docid=9ZyO3eYq84Rv7M&imgurl=http://www.dana.org/uploadedIma

(n.d.). Retrieved from http://www.reason.com/news/printer/35014.html

(n.d.). Retrieved from http://www.toyotageorgetown.com/qualdex.asp

(n.d.). Retrieved from http://www.customerservicemanager.com/how-to-keep-customers.htm

(n.d.). Retrieved from http://74.6.239.67/search/cache?ei=UTF-8&p=Walter+Buck+Swords+obituary&y=Search&fr=yfp-t-501&u=www.galesburg.com/columnists/x1151536461&w=walter+buck+swords+sword+obituary+obituaries&d=GpPcD_ReRYb-&icp=1&.intl=us

(n.d.). Retrieved from http://home.att.net/~coachthee/Archives/reciprocity.html

(n.d.). Retrieved from http://www.gamthaimassage.com/index_files/volunteer.htm

(n.d.). Retrieved from http://www.library.hbs.edu/hc/collections/kress/kress_img/adam_smith2.htm

(n.d.). Retrieved from http://lcweb2.loc.gov/cgi-bin/query/D?cstdy:6:./temp/~frd_1gy7::

(n.d.). Retrieved from http://lcweb2.loc.gov/cgi-bin/query/D?cstdy:2:./temp/~frd_1gy7::

Aaker, D. A. (1996). *Building Strong Brands*. New York, NY: The Free Press.

Abel, M., & Abel, M. (2007, April 20). *The Effects of a Sales Clerk's Smile on Consumer Perceptions and Behaviors*. Retrieved from pdfs.semanticscholar.org: https://pdfs.semanticscholar.org/e9a4/f2a5fdaff04754dde9040529a4b2ba40afcf.pdf?_ga=2.155112123.2012629694.1597013810-1290376172.1597013810

Adams, R. (n.d.). *Market Validation: Why Ready, Aim, Fire Beats Ready, Fire, Fire, Fire, Aim*. Retrieved from inc.com: https://www.inc.com/rob-adams/market-validation-new-book.html

Adrenal Medulla. (n.d.). Retrieved from wikipedia.com: https://en.wikipedia.org/wiki/Adrenal_medulla

Andreas, S. M., Faulkner, C. B., Gerling, K. P., Hallbom, T. M., McDonald, R. M., Schmidt, G. P., & Smith, S. (1994). *NLP, The New Technology of Achievement.* New York, New York: Harper Collins.

Art Dealers in the US industry statistics. (n.d.). Retrieved from ibisworld.com: https://www.ibisworld.com/united-states/market-research-reports/art-dealers-industry/

Bannon, L. (2009, September 18). *As Riches Fade, So Does Finance's Allure.* Retrieved from wallstreetjournal.com: https://www.wsj.com/articles/SB125322372695620969

Barboza, D. (2007, January 15). *China's 'Queen of Trash' finds riches in waste paper.* Retrieved from nytimes.com: https://www.nytimes.com/2007/01/15/business/worldbusiness/15iht-trash.4211783.html

Barrett, C. (2009, November 9). *Why praise employees?* Retrieved from humanergy.com: https://humanergy.com/why-praise-employees-isnt-pay-enough/

Berkman, H. W., Lindquist, J. D., & Sirgy, M. J. (1996). *Consumer Behavior.* Chicago, IL: NTC Business Books.

Best Places to Work 2020. (n.d.). Retrieved from Glassdoor.com: https://www.glassdoor.com/Award/Best-Places-to-Work-LST_KQ0,19.htm

Bottled Water. (n.d.). Retrieved from statista.com: https://www.statista.com/outlook/20010000/109/bottled-water/united-states

Campbell-Fortini, L. (1992). *Hitting the Sweet Spot.* Chicago, IL: The Copy Workshop.

Carlos Slim Helu. (n.d.). Retrieved from achievement.org: https://achievement.org/achiever/carlos-slim/

Carnegie, D. (1964). *How to Win Friends and Influence People.* New York, New York: Simon and Schuster.

Catecholamine. (n.d.). Retrieved from wikipedia.com: https://en.wikipedia.org/wiki/Catecholamine

CBS News. (2007). Retrieved from cbsnews.com: https://www.cbsnews.com/news/widow-leaves-chinese-restaurant-21m-tip/

Childers, D., & Grauds, C. (2005). *The Energy Prescription: Give Yourself Abundant Vitality with the Wisdom of America's Leading Natural Pharmacist.* New York, NY: Bantam Dell.

Cortisol. (n.d.). Retrieved from wikipedia: https://en.wikipedia.org/wiki/Cortisol

Customer. (n.d.). Retrieved from dictionary.com: https://www.dictionary.com/browse/customer

Cynicism link with heart disease. (2007, January 23). Retrieved from new.bbc.co.uk: http://news.bbc.co.uk/2/hi/6289847.stm

Diekmann, A. (n.d.). *The Power of Reciprocity.* Retrieved from socio.ethz.ch: https://socio.ethz.ch/content/dam/ethz/special-interest/gess/chair-of-sociology-dam/documents/articles/diekmann_jcr_2004.pdf

Displaced Aggression. (n.d.). Retrieved from psychology.iresearchnet.com: http://psychology.iresearchnet.com/social-psychology/antisocial-behavior/displaced-aggression/

Do couples truly share pain? Studies probe brain, empathy. (2004, Februar 19). Retrieved from usatoday.com: https://usatoday30.usatoday.com/news/health/2004-02-19-empathy_x.htm

Domestic Movie Theatrical Market Summary 1995 to 2020. (n.d.). Retrieved from the-numbers.com: https://www.the-numbers.com/market/

Duchenne smile. (n.d.). Retrieved from newscientist.com: https://www.newscientist.com/term/duchenne-smile/

Edmonds, M. (n.d.). *Are teenage brains really different from adult brains?* Retrieved from science.howstuffworks.com: https://science.howstuffworks.com/life/inside-the-mind/human-brain/teen-age-brain.htm

'Men Buy, Women Shop': The Sexes Have Different Priorities When Walking Down the Aisles. (2007, November 28). Retrieved from knowledge.wharton.upenn.edu: https://knowledge.wharton.upenn.edu/article/men-buy-women-shop-the-sexes-have-different-priorities-when-walking-down-the-aisles/

Ernst, J. (n.d.). *The History Behind The Mercedes-Benz Brand And The Three-Pointed Star.* Retrieved from theautochannel.com: http://www.theautochannel.com/news/2007/02/13/037004.html

Estimated revenue of U.S. software publishers from 2005 to 2019. (n.d.). Retrieved from statista.com: https://www.statista.com/statistics/184124/estimated-revenue-of-us-software-publishers-since-2005/

Farrah Gray. (n.d.). Retrieved from encyclopedia.com: https://www.encyclopedia.com/arts/educational-magazines/gray-farrah-1984

Fastenberg, D. (2011, August 11). *How Inner-City-Kid Farrah Gray Became A Millionaire By 14.* Retrieved from aol.com: https://www.

aol.com/2011/08/24/how-inner-city-kid-farrah-gray-became-a-millionaire-by-age-14/

Forbes. (2020, August 8). *#12 Carlos Slim*. Retrieved from Forbes: https://www.forbes.com/profile/carlos-slim-helu/#fed19e3646b3

Ford, H. (n.d.). *Ford, My Life and Work*.

Forswearing Greed. (2009, June 6). *The Economist*.

Fox, J. J. (1998). *How to Become CEO: Rules for Rising to the Top of Any Organization*. New York, NY: Hyperion.

Goldberg, C. (2008, March 3). *Brain scans support surprising differences in perception between Westerners and Asians*. Retrieved from archive.boston.com: http://archive.boston.com/news/science/articles/2008/03/03/cultural_insights/?page=2

Goleman, D. (2006, 2007). *Social Intelligence*. New York, New York: Bantam Dell.

Griffin, M. R. (n.d.). *Anger Control for Men*. Retrieved from webmd.com: https://www.webmd.com/men/features/anger-control-men

Grimm, R. J., Spring, K., & Dietz, N. (2007, April). *The Health Benefits of Volunteering*. Retrieved from nationalservice.gov: https://www.nationalservice.gov/pdf/07_0506_hbr.pdf

Grocery store sales in the United States from 1992 to 2019. (n.d.). Retrieved from statista.com: https://www.statista.com/statistics/197621/annual-grocery-store-sales-in-the-us-since-1992/

Gudykunst, W. B., & Kim, Y. Y. (1997). *Communicating with Strangers, An Approach to Intercultural Communication*. United States of America: McGraw-Hill.

Hafner, K. (2007, October 9). *Film Drop-Off Sites Fade Against Digital Cameras*. Retrieved from nytimes.com: https://www.nytimes.com/2007/10/09/business/09film.html

Hanson, R. (2007). *Empathy*. Retrieved from wisebrain.com: http://www.wisebrain.org/Empathy.pdf

Harlow, H. F. (1958). *The Nature of Love*. Retrieved from psychclassics.yorku.ca: http://psychclassics.yorku.ca/Harlow/love.htm

Harry Harlow. (n.d.). Retrieved from wikipedia.com: http://en.wikipedia.org/wiki/Harry_Harlow

Henry Ford. (n.d.). Retrieved from wikipedia: http://en.wikipedia.org/wiki/Henry_Ford#_note-6

Herper, M. (2011, April 19). *The Best-Selling Drugs In America.* Retrieved from Forbes.com: https://www.forbes.com/sites/matthewherper/2011/04/19/the-best-selling-drugs-in-america/#6e523b781993

Hooks, I. F., & Farry, K. A. (2001). *Customer-Centered Products.* New York, NY: AMACOM.

HP must pay $315 million to BSkyB. (2010, February 4). Retrieved from bizjournals.com: https://www.bizjournals.com/sanfrancisco/stories/2010/02/01/daily60.html?ana=yfcpc

Income. (n.d.). Retrieved from census.gov: https://www.census.gov/prod/2011pubs/12statab/income.pdf

Interesting Divorce Statistics, Facts, and Rate. (n.d.). Retrieved from fldivorce.com: https://fldivorce.com/blog/interesting-divorce-statistics-facts-and-rate/

J.D. Power and Associates Reports: HUMMER, Nissan and Scion Show Strong Improvement. (n.d.). Retrieved from theautochannel.com: http://www.theautochannel.com/news/2005/05/18/092157.html

Jane Elliott. (n.d.). Retrieved from wikipedia.com: https://en.wikipedia.org/wiki/Jane_Elliott

Kamikaze. (n.d.). Retrieved from wikipedia.com: https://en.wikipedia.org/wiki/Kamikaze

Kane, Y. I. (2009, January 15). *Apple's Jobs Takes Medical Leave.* Retrieved from The Wall Street Journal: https://www.wsj.com/articles/SB123196896984882901

Karoub, J. (n.d.). *Ford wins most vehicle quality awards.* Retrieved from usatoday.com: https://usatoday30.usatoday.com/money/economy/2007-06-06-1995544511_x.htm

Kiersz, A., & Rogers, T. N. (2020, July 29). *Jeff Bezos is about to defend his Amazon empire before Congress. Here's how the richest person in the world makes and spends his $178 billion fortune.* Retrieved from Business Insider: https://www.businessinsider.com/jeff-bezos-net-worth-life-spending-2018-8

King, N., & Mitchell, J. (2010, February 22). Toyota Document Hails Limited Recals. *Wall Street Journal*, p. 1.

Kodak kills Kodachrome film after 74 years. (n.d.). Retrieved from reuters.com: https://www.reuters.com/article/us-kodak-kodachrome/kodak-kills-kodachrome-film-after-74-years-idUSTRE55L3CZ20090622

Koh, K. B., Kim, D. K., Kim, S. Y., & Park, J. K. (2005). *The Relation Between Anger Expression, Depression, and Somatic Symptoms in Depressive Disorders and Somatoform Disorders.* Retrieved from psychiatrist.com: https://www.psychiatrist.com/JCP/article/Pages/2005/v66n04/v66n0411.aspx

Kotler, P., & Armstrong, G. (2008). *Principles of Marketing.* Upper Saddle River, New Jersey: Pearson Prentice Hall.

Laughter is the Best Medicine. (n.d.). Retrieved from helpguide.com: https://www.helpguide.org/articles/mental-health/laughter-is-the-best-medicine.htm

Laughter is the "Best Medicine" for Your Heart. (n.d.). Retrieved from livingscience.com: https://livingscience.ca/laughter-is-the-best-medicine-for-your-heart/

Laughter: The Best Medicine. (n.d.). Retrieved from psychologytoday.com: https://www.psychologytoday.com/us/articles/200504/laughter-the-best-medicine

Lichtenberg, R., & Stone, G. (1998). *Work Would Be Great If It Weren't For The People.* New York, NY: Hyperion.

Luks, A., & Payne, P. (1991, 2001). *The Healing Power of Doing Good.* Lincoln, NE: iUniverse.com.

Lumsden, G., & Lumsden, D. (1997). *Communicating in Groups and Teams: Sharing Leadership.* New York, NY: Wadsworth Publishing Company.

Maguire, W. (2007, August 19). *Six Reasons We Lose Customers.* Retrieved from ezinearticles.com: https://ezinearticles.com/?Six-Reasons-We-Lose-Customers&id=694711

Management Consulting in the US industry statistics. (n.d.). Retrieved from ibisworld.com: https://www.ibisworld.com/united-states/market-research-reports/management-consulting-industry/

Marquardt Beauty Analysis. (n.d.). Retrieved from beautyanalysis.com: https://www.beautyanalysis.com/articles/

Marquardt Beauty Analysis. (n.d.). Retrieved from beautyanalysis.com: https://www.beautyanalysis.com/articles/

Marton, J. (2015, May 6). *untappedcities.com.* Retrieved from untapped new york: https://untappedcities.com/2015/05/06/today-in-nyc-history-how-the-dutch-actually-bought-manhattan-the-long-version/

McConnell, C. R., & Brue, S. L. (1993). *Economics: Principles, Problems and Policies.* New York, New York: McGraw Hill.

Microsoft Encarta College Dictionary. (2001). New York, NY: Bloomsbury Publishing PLC.

Million, T., & Lerner, M. (n.d.). *The Hanbook of Psychology: Personality and Psychology.* Retrieved from https://books.google.com/books?id=lBXf1slZBDwC&pg=PA393&lpg=PA393&dq=(DePaulo,+Brittingham,+and+Kaiser+1983;+Eisenberger,+Cotterell,+and+Marvel,+1987;+Regan,+1971)&source=bl&ots=kY3_0mShbp&sig=ACfU3U084kO_MatroznJw2tk2iuNQqNf6A&hl=en&sa=X&ved=2ahUKEwi9zf3

Myers, D. G. (1993). *Social Psychology.* New York, New York: McGraw-Hill.

Nike's Heritage. (n.d.). Retrieved from xroads.virgina.edu: http://xroads.virginia.edu/~CLASS/am483_97/projects/hincker/nikhist.html

Papadoloulos, A. (2020, August). *CEO World Magazine.* Retrieved from ceoworld.biz: https://ceoworld.biz/2020/08/08/rich-list-index-top-500-billionaires-in-the-world-meet-the-richest-people-on-earth-2020/

Rapport. (n.d.). Retrieved from merrian-websters.com: http://www.merriam-webster.com/dictionary/rapport

Rath, T., & Clifton, D. O. (204). *How Full Is Your Bucket?* New York, NY: Gallup Press.

Reichheld, F. (2001). *The Loyalty Effect: The Hidden Force Behind Growth, Profits, and Lasting Value.* United States of America: Harvard Business School Press.

Ruth, A., Wysocki, A., Farnsworth, D., & Clark, J. L. (n.d.). *Top Sellers: Characteristics of a Superior Salesperson.* Retrieved from edis.ifas.ufl.edu: https://edis.ifas.ufl.edu/pdffiles/SN/SN00400.pdf

Save the babies: American public health reform and the prevention of infant mortality, 1850–1929 . (n.d.). Retrieved from ncbi.nlm.nih.gov: https://www.ncbi.nlm.nih.gov/pmc/articles/PMC1036505/

Selfridges. (n.d.). Retrieved from wikipedia.com: https://en.wikipedia.org/wiki/Selfridges

Selig, M. (2016, May 25). *The 9 Superpowers of Your Smile.* Retrieved from psychologytoday.com: https://www.psychologytoday.com/us/blog/changepower/201605/the-9-superpowers-your-smile

Shirouzu,, N. (2010, March 2). Toyota Rues Excessive Profit Focus. *The Wall Street Journal*, p. 3.

Simonson, I., & Ofir, C. (2005). *The Effect of Stating Expectations on Customer Satisfaction and Shopping Experience.* Retrieved from gsb.stanford.edu: https://www.gsb.stanford.edu/faculty-research/working-papers/effect-stating-expectations-customer-satisfaction-shopping

Smith, A. (1759). *The Theory of Moral Sentiments.* England.

Smith, A. (2003). *The Wealth of Nations.* Bantam Classics.

sociopolitical. (n.d.). Retrieved from merriam-webster.com: https://www.merriam-webster.com/dictionary/sociopolitical

Soniak, M. (2012, October 2). *Was Manhattan Really Bought for $24?* Retrieved from mentalfloss.com: https://www.mentalfloss.com/article/12657/was-manhattan-really-bought-24

Sonne, P. (2010, January 26). *BSkyB Wins Legal Victory Against EDS.* Retrieved from wsj.com: https://www.wsj.com/articles/SB10001424052748703906204575027303086931726

Stibich, M. (2020, February 4). *Top 10 Reasons You Should Smile Every Day.* Retrieved from verywellmind.com: https://www.verywellmind.com/top-reasons-to-smile-every-day-2223755

Stress Related Illinesses. (n.d.). Retrieved from humanillinesses.com: http://www.humanillnesses.com/original/Se-Sy/Stress-Related-Illness.html

Swanson's Unwritten Rules. (n.d.). Retrieved from usatoday.com: https://usatoday30.usatoday.com/money/companies/management/2006-04-14-ceos-waiter-rule_x.htm

The Psychology of Safety Handbook. (n.d.). Retrieved from https://books.google.com/books?id=504MGltUZE0C&pg=PA375&lpg=PA375&dq=reciprocity+norm+AND+christmas+card+experiment&source=web&ots=s5acru-ZQ-&sig=JDoAbW_YUdSSPRsj14D3yHud0Q0&hl=en&sa=X&oi=book_result&resnum=2&ct=result#v=onepage&q=reciprocity%20norm%20AND

Theory of Mind. (n.d.). Retrieved from wikipedia.com: https://en.wikipedia.org/wiki/Theory_of_mind

Thor. (2006, December 14). *Bah-humbug: Science is proving there is a Helper's High*. Retrieved from sciencebuzz.com: http://www.sciencebuzz.org/blog/bah_humbug_science_is_proving_there_is_a_helpers_high

Trout, J. (2006, July 3). *Peter Drucker on Marketing*. Retrieved from Forbes: http://www.forbes.com/2006/06/30/jack-trout-on-marketing-cx_jt_0703drucker.html

Ulrich, K. T., & Eppinger, S. D. (2004). *Product Design and Development*. New York, NY: Mcgraw-Hill.

Waitress Gets $50,000 From Cranky Customer. (n.d.). Retrieved from http://www.nbcnews.com/id/22424002/ns/us_news-wonderful_world/t/waitress-gets-car-cranky-texan/

Wang, Z., MAO, H., LI, Y. J., & LIU, F. (2017). Smile Big or Not? Effects of Smile Intensity on Perceptions of Warmth and Competence. *Journal of Consumer Research*, 787-805.

Yahoo! Finance. (n.d.). Retrieved from finance.yahoo.com: http://finance.yahoo.com/q/is?s=NKE+Income+Statement&annual

Zebrowitz, L., & Rhodes, G. (2002). *Facial Attractiveness: Evolutionary, Cognitive, and Social Perspectives (International Perspectives on Individual Differences*. Westport, CT: Ablex Publishing.

Zhivotovskaya , E. (2008, September 27). *SMILE AND OTHERS SMILE WITH YOU: HEALTH BENEFITS, EMOTIONAL CONTAGION, AND MIMICRY.* Retrieved from positivepsychologynew.com: https://positivepsychologynews.com/news/emiliya-zhivotovskaya/200809271036

Ziglar, Z. (1984). *Zig Ziglar's Secrets of Closting the Sale*. United States of America: Fleming H. Revell Company.

Index

Y

Z

CPSIA information can be obtained
at www.ICGtesting.com
Printed in the USA
BVHW030735060421
604309BV00011B/659/J